THE MEDICAL ETHIC

MEDICINE AS A SOCIAL SCIENCE

RUSSELL NOBLETT, MD

CITIOFBOOKS, INC.
3736 Eubank NE Suite A1
Albuquerque, NM 87111-3579
www.citiofbooks.com
Hotline: 1 (877) 389-2759
Fax: 1 (505) 930-7244

Ordering Information:
Quantity sales. Special discounts are available on quantity purchases by corporations, associations, and others. For details, contact the publisher at the address above.

Printed in the United States of America.
ISBN-13:   Paperback   979-8-90124-220-9
                eBook   979-8-90124-222-3
                Hardback   979-8-90124-221-6

Library of Congress Control Number: 2026905874

DEDICATION

To the poet, Carmella Santorelli

CONTENTS

ACKNOWLEDGEMENTS

I wish to acknowledge the guidance I received from the late Prof Richard Owsley, Chairman of the Dept of Philosophy at the University of North Texas during my pre-medical training years. As a student of Karl Jaspers and Edmund Husserl, his instruction and counsel helped me to understand the doctor-patient relationship, and to know the direction to look as I explored the nature of medical decision making.

I gratefully acknowledge the editorial review and advice of Dr. Susan Molumphy, PhD, my colleague in practice and residency education over the last twenty years. Her learned understanding of medical science and her preternatural gift as a counselor to the creative mind were of great value to me in the protracted work ofwriting this book. She also contributed her expertise in the use of AI tools to create pictorial illustrations at key points throughout this work.

I affectionately acknowledge the review and advice of the poet and author, Carmella Santorelli, who in the final years of the composition of this work became an essential philosophical and spiritual sounding board for its main themes.

Finally, I am grateful to the dozens of colleagues, consultants and medicine residents, whose impromptu late-night conversations on the wards and in the doctors lounge over the last twenty years served as a laboratory in which to test the ideas in this book against the critical minds of doctors engaged in the daily care of patients.

PREFACE

"One of the essential qualities of the clinician is interest in humanity, for the secret of the care of the patient is incaring for the patient."

- Dr. Francis Peabody, Harvard Medical School, 1926

The tension between the science of medicine and what is called the "art" of medicine, that is, between objective medical decision making in practice based on the technical terms and tools of medical science, versus bedside care informed by subjective input from the doctor-patient relationship, is as old as Hippocrates.

However, this tension grew rapidly during the latter20th and early 21st centuries in concert with the new computerization of medicine, coming to a head with the emergence of artificial intelligence in machine learning. From its initial status as a mere philosophical musing with little practical consequence, this conflict between the science and the art of medicine grew into a stumbling block for the clinician, and a worrisome misdirection for medicine as a social institution.

It is commonplace now for the physician to enter an exam room or a hospital room and to address a computer screen rather than the patient. Just a few decades ago, when I trained as an internist, this would have been considered a small outrage and a scandal, probably drawing a reprimand from the attending physician. But today the mantra of "evidence-based" medicine, harnessed by the new sophisticated computer tools, presents itself as the sufficient condition, the end-in-itself, of quality medical decision making. There remains little reason to talk to the patient.

However, as every experienced clinician knows,and as new young doctors risk discovering too late, an exclusive reliance on rigorous evidence-based medicine eventually and inevitably will find the clinician simply "rigorously wrong" with regard to the patient. That is, there remains a subjective element of medical decision making that is essential for the effective formulation and deployment of the medical decision. This humanistic component is essential also for the effective deployment of medicine as a social institution.

The physician retains a sense of this subjective element. She knows that it is essential to her role as a doctor. But it is not accommodated by the evidence-based model of care that now drives her schedule.

The exclusive claims of medical technology did not present such an impediment to care in the time of Dr. Peabody; for, compared to today, there was relatively little that could be done for a patient beyond support. Therefore, ample time remained for attention to bedside manner. This left space for spontaneous eruption of a creative response to the patient's peculiar needs.

Now, however, after several decades of exponential growth in medical technology, that claims for itself the role of final arbiter in the medical decision, the doctor-patient relationship must compete for time and mental space. Without an alternate model of medical decision-making - one that argues for the dependence of rigorous evidence-based medicine on the clinician's subjective impression - the clinician is left with no moral support, no philosophical wedge, in defense of her inclination to return to the doctor-patient interaction.

It seems that there remains only one solution. In order to show that medicine exists to engage the human condition at a level that is more fundamental than the tools of medical science, one must demonstrate that these tools of medical science, though they appear given as the elements of the medical decision, are in fact mere artifacts, intermediary products of a more fundamental and creative response to the milieu of the doctor-patient relationship.

This must include showing how clinical data, that appear "given" as evidence, are in fact constituted for an end beyond themselves, and how the logical necessity of their evidence-based formulations confers utility, but not final truth, to the objective formulation. One must see this objective process as a creative response to some deeper human end, and one must identify this deeper humanistic agenda that the creative process serves.

Finally, one must address a question that is posed by the emergence of artificial intelligence as a tool of clinical decision making. Is there an essential feature of decision making that is exclusive to consciousness, so that the clinician cannot simply defer to machine learning when addressing a patient's need? Specifically, is there a creative interface between the brain and the cosmos that, though it can be simulated by an AI agent, cannot be reproduced, such that it must be permitted to remain independent as the arbiter of clinical decision making?

By demonstrating the steps of this creative process,

one hopes to deflect the inclination to reduce medicine to the objective terms of mere medical science and information technology. One hopes to clear the way to see instead directly to the human agenda that they serve, and that herein we will call the "medical ethic."

CHAPTER I:
A PHILOSOPHICAL MEMOIR

"Then in one vast thousandfold thought I could think you up to where thinking ends. I could possess you, even for the brevity of a smile, to offer you to all that lives, in gladness." [5]

- Rainer Maria Rilke, Book of Hours I, 7, 1905

An intellectual autobiography

It might not seem so initially, but this philosophical narrative is a personal memoir. It recounts the efforts of a practicing physician to understand what he is "doing" as a doctor. The questions posed are practical, but the answers require engaging fundamental issues in the natural and social sciences, that the typical physician will encounter in the course of a career.

I started some decades ago, during my pre-medical training years as a college student in philosophy, with two questions: What is the structure of medical decision making, and what role does medicine play as a social institution in the larger human agenda?

The reduction of medical decision making to the objective terms of medical science will not do for this inquiry. These terms evolve constantly, and they replace themselves continuously over time. Something more basic and permanent is manifesting in the doctor-patient relationship that cannot be grasped alone by the rigidly objective terms of medical science, though these are in fact the tools whereby we achieve our end.

What is this deeper end, this human agenda, that we will call the medical ethic, and how do the objective tools of medical science emerge to satisfy it?

In this exploration I have chosen not to take the solipsistic approach of a physician recounting anecdotes from his medical practice, though my observations will serve as illustrations throughout this narrative. Instead, I have attempted to harness the insights of thinkers from various disciplines as they pertain to the creative and social features of scientific thinking in general.

Thereby I have sought to situate medicine within the context of a larger inquiry taking place in our time within the natural sciences regarding their creative and humanistic foundation.

In the first four chapters of this book I will describe in detail the steps of the creative process of medical decision making. In the last chapter I will describe a metadata model for the design of clinical computer decision tools that facilitate this creative process. This model is intended to serve as a practical illustration of the philosophical concepts described herein.

The role of consciousness

This journey has taken me well beyond the routine terms of medicine as it is practiced traditionally. For instance, since the doctor-patient relationship, in one form or another, is characteristic of every recorded society, I assume that it cannot be simply a product oflocal custom. Instead, it must represent some basic feature of human consciousness, so that it manifests necessarily as a social institution in all times and places.

For this reason, the nature of consciousness itself has been of interest to me. Regarding this, I have been drawn to the proposition of the philosopher, Thomas Nagel, who argues that the propensity for consciousness must have existed in the beginning of the universe, "in consequence of the already-existing properties of the fundamental particles." [1]

This is a version of what is called the "anthropic principle" in cosmology. The anthropic principle is not a philosophical proposition. It simply is an observation that serves as a heuristic tool in scientific investigation.

Universal Consciousness. *Susan Saandholland on Midjourney*

That is, an anthropic principle facilitates scientific inquiry by posing the obvious fact that the conditions of the early universe must have been those necessary to produce its manifest products, such as life. For instance, one must assume that the primordial stellar furnace was sufficient for the fusion of helium nuclei necessary to create the carbon nucleus, and so the organic chemical processes that are necessary for what we call life.

In so doing, however, this anthropic principle also implies that life, and so consciousness, reflect the fundamental nature of the cosmos. This is not so much a controversial proposition. It just is one that might not otherwise come to attention as a first principle when considering the nature of consciousness, and of medical decision making, as it derives therein.

Even if consciousness is a random result of the first quantum fluctuations and, following long thereafter, a "mistake" of evolution, it still must mirror essential features of the cosmos. Simply in that it exists it reflects the cosmic structure in its possibilities, and on this countit has cosmic significance. It remains for us to describe this significance and how it manifests in practice.

The brain as evolved conduit

Similarly, I have been intrigued by the seminal efforts of the Nobel laureate physicist, Roger Penrose, toaccount for consciousness in terms of the quantum potential of the micro-tubular infrastructure of the brain.

Micro-tubules are known already in cell biology

as the non-neurologic molecular structures that guide complex activity, such as the migrating of chromosomes in the cell divisions of meiosis and mitosis. Penrose hypothesized that this same microtubular infrastructure, as it is found in the brain, might similarly be more fundamental to consciousness than the neuronal networkthat it subsumes, through its peculiar molecular structurethat makes quantum processes plausible, such as entanglement and coherence.

This hypothesis is interesting not because of any experimental results thus far, not because it has proven consciousness to be a function of quantum processes, but because it begs a much more fundamental question. Quantum processes make it plausible to imagine the brain not as an insular substrate of consciousness, sealedoff from the rest of the universe, but as an evolved quantum-level conduit through which the universe constitutes awareness of itself, manifesting as individual consciousness and thereby giving to consciousness a cosmic meaning. As Carl Sagan famously proposed, "we are a way for the cosmos to know itself." [2]

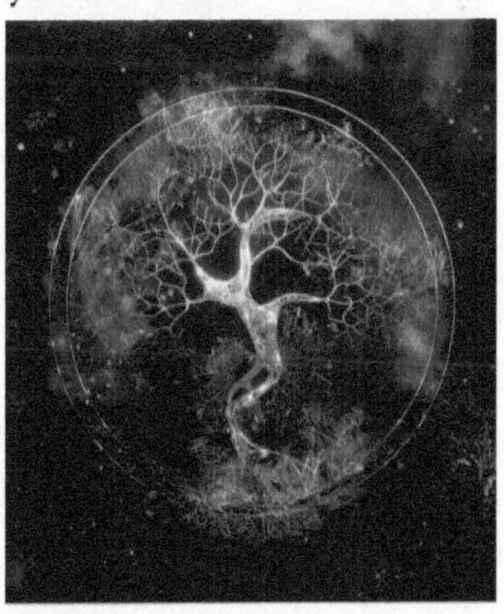

Quantum Connection. *Susan Saandholland on Midjourney*

If this is true, then the universe is not merely the objective content of consciousness, that is the things we think about. Rather, it is the substance of consciousness. Consciousness is the universe perceiving itself through the agency of the evolved brain, and in the limited anthropic way that the brain makes possible. This renders a cosmic relevance to medical decision making.

This has implications for what we call empathy and intersubjectivity, as they manifest for instance in the doctor-patient relationship. If we take each individual consciousness as an instance of the universe knowing itself, then consciousness in all instances is an active manifestation of a common source. Intersubjectivity is a dialogue with a shared reference. When we speak or listen to each other it is with regard to this common source. At this higher level we know what the other is thinking because we share this content, even as we accommodate for variation in dialogue. Herein is the ontological foundation of intersubjectivity and empathy.

Interdisciplinary sources

I have sought to put more flesh on these notions for the sake of their application to medicine. The result is a narrative that integrates different disciplines as they pertain to medicine. To help in this exploration I have harnessed minds from divergent fields as they pertain to the nature of science and society, and thus to objective medical decision making and to its humanistic agenda.

In particular, I will make frequent reference to the thought of Sir Arthur Eddington, the early 20th century astrophysicist, whose demonstration of the deflection of light by the gravitational field of the sun was taken as an early confirmation of the theory of general relativity.

Eddington helped to popularize the new theory of relativity to the English-speaking world at a time when everything German was suspect due to two world wars.

His focus was not just on explaining the theory of relativity but in explaining the implications of relativity theory for the nature of scientific thought in general. In particular, he described the influence of the anthropic contingencies of knowing on the creation of scientific theory. On this count his ideas have relevance for our project. We can begin to see how objective medical decision making relies upon the subjective milieu of the doctor-patient relationship.

I also will refer to the 20th century philosopher-theologian Paul Tillich, whose notion of man's relation to man and to the universe was born in the same era as Eddington.

Tillich's notion of man's response to open-ended possibility in the foundation of the human condition helped to free social thought from the naive determinism of the 18th century enlightenment and the nihilism of the 19th and 20th centuries. For example, in a passage that ultimately applies to the doctor-patient relationship, Tillich describes the existential foundation of love in terms of open-ended possibility...

Love is always love; that is its static and absolute side. But love is always dependent on that which is loved, and therefore it is unable to force finite elements on finite existence in the name of an assumed absolute. The absoluteness of love is its power to go into the concrete situation, to discover what is demanded by the predicament of the concrete to which it turns. [73]

The perspective of open-ended possibility

These two thinkers, Eddington and Tillich, will help us to clarify a theory of medical decision making as the formulation of objective knowledge in response to the subjective perception of human possibility as it is apprehended directly in the doctor-patient relationship.

Specifically, I will argue that perception of possibility, experienced as a mundane feature of all of awareness, is a fundamental level of consciousness. It underlies all cognitive activity in our grasp of the world in objective form. From this ontological beginning we will describe the purpose and the creative structure of medical decision making.

We will see also that positing open-ended possibility as the foundation of the medical decision subverts the popular notion of "evidence-based medicine." This is because evidence-based medicine presumes that objective data and logical rigor derived from them are the given elements, and the final arbiters, of the medical decision. However, we will see, from the perspective of possibility theory, that in medical practice, as in love, this naive assumption often leaves the clinician simply "rigorously wrong" with regard to the patient.

The underlying perspectival nature of medical decision making, driven by the direct apprehension of human possibility in the doctor-patient relationship, is rendered opaque to the decision maker by this naive theory of evidence-based medicine. With the help of insights from Tillich and Eddington and others, we will seek to rescue medicine from this blind alley.

Molecular biology as end in itself

For example, in 1985 at the University of Texas Medical School in Dallas, my fellow students and I werethrilled to learn that two of our beloved professors had won the Nobel Prize in medicine for discovering the molecular receptor for cholesterol. This set the stage for the study and design of new medicines for the treatment of atherosclerotic heart disease.

This molecular discovery, and others like it before and since then, made it appear that the ultimate goal of medicine lies in describing the molecular structure of human physiology and pathophysiology. As the famed 20th century molecular biologist, Jacques Monod, had said, molecular biology is central, since "of all the disciplines it is the one that endeavors to go most directly to the heart of the problem before that of 'human nature' can even be framed in other than metaphysical terms." [146]

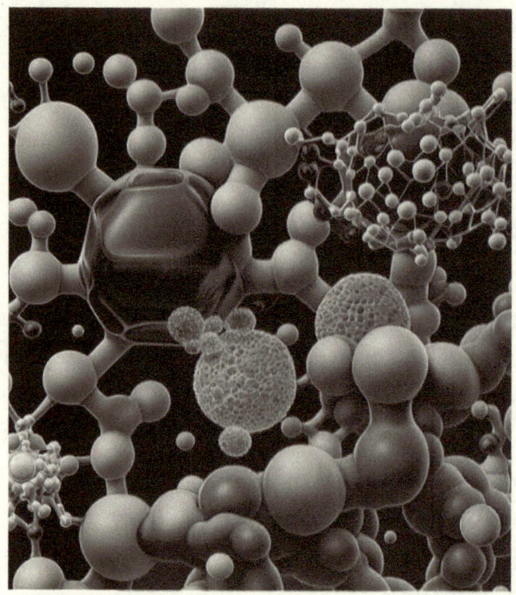

Molecular Paradigm. *Susan Saandholland on Midjourney*

Thus, the researcher and the clinician come to feel that they are the passive discoverers and dutiful practitioners of molecular formulations, that are taken asthe given elements of health and illness and of medical decision making.

Yet something is missing in this view. As we will see, it makes a difference whether one conceives of these molecular formulations as the discovered ends in themselves, as Monod proposed, versus as the formulated perspectival means to an end beyond themselves, in the grasp and actualization of human possibility. This latter view permits reconnection to empathy in the doctor-patient relationship.

The mythological function of "disease"

After winning the Nobel prize, and in their chapter on medical genetics, Drs Brown and Goldstein made an interesting observation: They noted that about half of the genes, and thus half of the protein products, thatexist in any one individual are different from those in the majority of the population. [30]

The significance of this observation for our purposes is that the occurrence of genetic variation in itself does not warrant the designation of "disease." For example, people with hereditary large noses are not ill and do not need to be cured. Rather, the designation of disease is warranted by the subjective significance of a specific genetic variation to the patient.

This is belied by the mythological function of the notion of disease. That is, the word "disease" draws the attention of the clinician to the human possibility that it grasps in the negative, as absent, so as to direct the clinician to its actualization in terms of a "cure." So, the designation of "disease" is a choice. It is an existential decision regarding what features of human possibility are felt subjectively to warrant actualization.

This decision begins and ends with apprehension ofhuman possibility in the doctor-patient relationship. The objective formulation is an intermediate and utilitarian step. It is neither given nor is it the end in itself.

For instance, certain mutations in the gene for the cholesterol receptor protein that Brown and Goldstein discovered manifest as the phenotype called "autosomal dominant hypercholesterolemia," and it will result in premature coronary artery disease. But there are other variations in the same gene (called "polymorphisms") that are said to be normal variations, though they also contribute to susceptibility to poor outcome. [31]

In other words, the cutoff for what gene variation is said to constitute a "disease" and what will be called a "normal variation" is a function of the subjective impression of its utility to the patient, and to medical theory, and to its social ramifications as well.

Another example of this existential choice in clinical practice is the onset of urinary incontinence in the elderly. Should one consider incontinence to be a normal feature of aging, or should it be considered a disease? This decision is influenced by the fact that incontinence often can be reversed. It can be "cured." Therefore, it is taught to the medical student as a moral obligation to call incontinence a disease.

As we will see later, the moral sense in general, and in medicine in particular, similarly originates in the awareness of responsibility for perceived human possibility.

The proposition that the designation of "disease" is perspectival might meet initially with indignation. A debater might protest that, "Certainly you are not proposing that designating conditions such as diabetes mellitus or ovarian cancer as disease is a matter merely of perspective!" But this indignation itself is an illustration of the perspectival element.

As a thought experiment, one might consider the example of Down Syndrome. This genetic variation is associated with mental retardation, heart malformation, and immune deficiency, but also with a charming disposition of personality that tends to manifest as unconditional positive regard of others. Should this latterquality, being the result of a genetic mutation, be considered disease?

We revolt against this on first impression. We might argue that it is just because this isolated trait likely would contribute to survival that it should not be considered a "disease." But, though this might be true, our indignation at calling it "disease" is not driven by an anticipation of survival value. Rather, our indignation is driven by an assertion of existential choice regarding what features we should wish to see survive as human nature.

The point is that it is a choice. The designation of "disease" serves an end beyond itself in response to the subjective impression of possibility.

The anthropic origin of objective science

As our exploration develops, we will discover not only that every objective medical decision originates as acreative choice, but that the objective terms themselves of the medical decision, such as the "molecules" of molecular biology, emerge as anthropic tools to serve this creative end.

That is, these terms come into being to accommodate the anthropic contingencies of knowing, such as the need to grasp possibility as objects for the subject. As Eddington said, our sensory equipment has a selective effect, so that whatever we apprehend is apprehended "in a way for which our intellectual equipment has made provision." [35]

This realization steers us away from the illusion of evidence-based formulation as the given foundation of the medical decision. It alerts us instead to an origin that requires subjective impression for objective formulation.In the end, it is as Eddington observed…

We have found that where science has progressed thefarthest, the mind has but regained from nature that which the mind has put into nature. We have found a strange footprint on the shores of the unknown. We have devised profound theories, one after another, to account for its origin. At last we have succeeded in reconstructing the creature that made the footprint. And lo! It is our own. [34]

Molecular biology comes into being as an anthropic, and thus perspectival, window. It is reality as the knowercan know it, within the evolved bounds of the perceivingbrain. It does not represent the limits of reality, but the limits of the knowing of reality.

For instance, the concept of "interactive molecules" serves the need to grasp perceived possibility as objects of analysis that have uniform units of measure and the technical means of navigating toward a desired end. As molecular biology therein applies to all of subjective knowing, it appears to apply to all of knowable reality.

That is, it appears as an element of reality itself. It is not surprising then that it is taken to be given as the intended end in itself.

This acknowledgement of its anthropic origin helps to maintain awareness of the existential ground of possibility that it serves, and to remind the user to return to this ground as the creative imperative requires. One is less inclined to defer to objective formulation due to its mere objectivity. One comes to see objectivity as a tool and an artifact. One remains mindful of the subjective milieu of the doctor-patient relationship from which it arises.

We will have achieved this perspective fully only when we have shown that medical science, by appearing to the user as the objective end in itself, is thereby serving an end beyond itself - in precipitating the subject-object interaction whereby possibility is actualized - that is, when objective medical science is understood to function as a myth.

The humanistic agenda of medicine

The clinician, when dealing with diabetes mellitus for example, must understand that it is a disease not becauseof an elevated blood glucose, but because of the subjective meaning of an elevated blood glucose for the patient. It is at this level that the clinician must engage with the patient if he or she is to function as a doctor.

The courage of the physician to step into this horizon of open-ended possibility is an instance of, and a paradigm of, the agenda of medicine as a human institution. The social agenda of medicine then is the apprehension of human possibility for the sake of its actualization.

As Tillich said, the purpose of social interaction isthe actualization of the "potentialities of man as man," sothat "humanity is attained by self-determination and other-determination in mutual dependence." [13]

This awareness has the capacity to precipitate an existential crisis at the sociological level that is similar to the individual clinician's inclination to withdraw from this daunting responsibility when it first is encountered.

The recognition of open-ended possibility can appear as an "abyss of nothingness" if one anticipates finding a given meaning instead. As Nietzsche said, the mind, upon realizing that its familiar truth is not the truth in itself, will assume that there is simply "no truth" to be found. Nietzsche described this nihilistic inclination as a pathologic transition stage [76].

With courage, and in time, and with a receptive mind, this abyss of nothingness is recognized instead as a "horizon of possibility." Paralysis then is replaced with an impulse for creative response. As Ortega y Gasset described in the early 20th century, one recognizes that this "horizon ever open to all contingencies, constitutes authentic life, the true fullness of our existence." [74]

Not only does the physician then discover the true agenda of the medical decision in recognizing the primal nature of man, but society discovers the true agenda of medicine as social institution. Man is no longer reduced to a project of mere physiology, for physiology is now understood as an anthropic tool with which to graspman's deeper meaning in possibility.

Physical perception as limitation of the brain

I will lay the groundwork for this analysis with an assumption that I believe to be held in some manner by most philosophers of natural science today: that the reduction of reality to a "physical" world reflects a limitation of the brain, rather than a limitation of reality.

This reflects how the brain has evolved as that organ through which the universe comes to know itself. This manifests as consciousness, and it takes the form of an objective world existing apart-from a subjective knower in the emerging theater of the mind.

The science of consciousness itself is subject to this self-imposed limitation, taking the form of a physiological study of the brain. As Bertrand Russell quipped, "What the physiologist sees when he examinesa brain is in the physiologist, not in the brain he isexamining." [64]

In the end, the phenomenon of life touches upon a process that no single metaphor can encompass. As Eddington said, "It would be unreasonable to limit our thought of nature to what can be comprised in sense-pictures." [54] This is our natural anthropic myopia.

The universe existed before the mind. It does not require the mind for its reality. However, it is through the mind that the universe comes to know itself as an objective world set apart from a subjective knower.

So, for instance, one might ask whether the moon existed before there was an objective knower to observe it. The answer is neither yes nor no. Rather, it is that what we call "the moon" is the way the universe has evolved to perceive itself, as an object for, and apart- from, the subject in mind. As Eddington said...

The actuality of Nature is like the beauty of Nature. We can scarcely describe the beauty of a landscape as non-existent when there is no conscious being to witness it; but it is through consciousness that we can attribute a meaning to it. And so it is with the actuality of the world. If actuality means "known to the mind" then it is a purely subjective character of the world; to make it objective we must substitute "knowable to mind." [3]

A common ground for knower and known

The duality of mind and body, that Rene Descartes codified in his formulation "cogito ergo sum," as a foundation for scientific knowledge, set the stage for the physical reductionism of medicine. The physical object existing apart from the knowing subject is taken thereby to be given as the intended end of the scientific decision. This dualistic formulation is valuable as a utilitarianmyth for science, but it remains a problematic obstacle to exploring the common ground of knower and known.

This is because, at the most fundamental level of consciousness, the perceiving subject has a background awareness of his participation in a common domain that he shares with the perceived world. As Tillich said, the self perceives itself as "a part of the world that it has as its world." [11] Nevertheless, the subject and object are made to appear separate from each other in the theater of the mind, as a product of the evolved brain. This results in the subject-object interaction that we recognize as objective science.

The product of this subject-object interaction, and therefore its manifest purpose, is the actualization of the domain of possibility, that is the common ground of subject and object, and that is the ultimate goal of science.

The scientist, in her role as the perceiving subject, presumes the object as it appears in front of her to be the aim of science. But it is through the resulting subject-object interaction that the aim of science is ultimately accomplished - that is the grasp and actualization of the domain of possibility. It is for this reason that the object must be "anthropic" in form. It comes into being for the purpose of interaction with the subject.

Acknowledgement of a common ground for the knowing self and the knowable world is ancient. For instance, a central teaching of the Buddha is that suffering in its deepest sense, called "dukkha" in Sanskrit, is a result of the illusion that the self exists separate from the cosmos that it perceives.

Buddhist meditation is conceived as a method to deconstruct this erroneous sense of a separate self, and tothereby permit a return to awareness of participation in this deeper unity. This sense of a shared ground with the object characterizes also the milieu of the doctor-patient relationship. This is captured ontologically by Tillich in terms that might apply to medicine...

When we become aware of the unity of all beings, something happens to us. The fact that others do not have changes the character of our having... Our becoming aware of the fact that others who could have developed into full human beings did not, changes our state of full humanity. Their early death, their early or late disintegration, brings to our own personal life and health a continuous risk, a dying that is not yet death, a disintegration that is not yet destruction. In every death we encounter, something of us dies, and in every disease, something of us tends towards disintegration. [25]

The cosmic role of the knowing subject

Each instance of consciousness, in the act of perceiving the cosmos, is an instance of the cosmos perceiving itself. This does not mean that the individual self continues after death, as in the persistence of an eternal soul. It means that consciousness in the present is an emergent manifestation of an eternal order, through the constituting action of the brain.

This recognition of consciousness as manifestation of the universe is facilitated by reductive meditation, or simply through contemplating the terms of the new physics of relativity and quantum theory, in which the conditions of perception are found to be integral to the perceived object. As Eddington said, "No complete view can be obtained so long as we separate our consciousness from the world of which it is a part." [23]

This affirmation of a common substance for mind and matter finds its way into the great historical systems of cosmology, manifesting in what Aldus Huxley called the "perineal philosophy." As Eddington said...

If I were to try to put into words the essential truth revealed in the mystic experience, it would be that our minds are not apart from the world; and the feelings that we have of gladness and melancholy and our yet deeper feelings are not of ourselves alone, but are glimpses of a reality transcending the narrow limits of our particular consciousness - that the harmony and beauty of the face of Nature is at root one with the gladness that transfigures the face of man. [24]

Stepping back from the Cartesian duality

By identifying the domain of possibility as the common ground of subject and object, we are able to step back from their absolute separation in the Cartesian duality.

We can begin to describe, in terms of possibility itself, the creative process whereby the object comes into being for the subject. Then we can understand how the subjective milieu of the doctor-patient relationship serves as a necessary predicate for objective medical decision making.

This background awareness of possibility brings with it the sense of an abiding "veil" in consciousness, as a "glass through which we see darkly."

This veil is simply the brain's awareness of its own functional limitation. It is the divide between the background domain of possibility, in which the brain knows itself as a manifestation, and the world that it creates in its objectifying activity - that is, in its grasp of this same domain as if it were an objective world existing apart-from a knowing subject in mind.

This pre-objective side of this veil must remain a "mystery," for it can be experienced only as awareness itself. As Eddington said, "When we try to get behind the wording, we find nothing to support the view that awareness is a subject-object relation, or even a subject-transitive relation." [4]

In ancient Buddhism this domain is called the ineffable "Suchness," a word chosen because it signifies the limitation of words. Our notion of the domain of possibility therefore is a defiled version of Suchness. It presumes to describe this pre-objective domain as if it were an object for our analysis.

The notion of "possibility" therefore is a metaphor that captures how this pre-objective domain presents itself in consciousness - as a domain that exists for the purpose of actualization. That is, it exists as possibility. What we call "possibility" has an infinite and much more rich structure, that is worked out in terms of "what is possible." In this, its core nature for us, as possibility, is foundational to all objective knowing.

Possibility as source of objective knowledge

This primal domain of possibility is recognized as the source of objective knowledge. Kant referred to this pre-objective consciousness as the "transcendental apperception." It drives the objectifying activity of the brain, to grasp features of possibility as if they were in fact objects apart-from the subject. In this way objective knowledge comes into being.

The fundamental unity of the knowing subject and the known object never dissolves. However, awareness of it recedes into the background of consciousness. The illusion of an absolute distinction between the knowing subject and a known objective world persists in mind as the constituting action of the brain. It is in this way that objective knowledge can be said to be "about" the universe, for it is the universe knowing itself through theobjectifying activity of the brain.

The created object appears to the subject as a way of measuring the universe apart from the perspectival impurity of "subjective" input. However, as Eddington observed, "Any apparatus used to measure the world is itself part of the world, so that the natural gauge represents the world as self-gauging." [12] In this way, every objective measure is necessarily anthropic; for itis the universe self-gauging through the agency of the evolved brain.

Nevertheless, the project of objective science, in physics as well as in medicine, appears to the user as a process entirely separate from subjective influence. As Eddington pointed out...

Physical science has seemed to occupy a domain of reality which is self-sufficient, pursuing its course independently of and indifferent to that which a voice within us asserts to be a higher reality... It is in this background that our own mental consciousness lies; and here, if anywhere, we may find a Power greater than but akin to consciousness. [16]

We have identified this background "power" as the perceived domain of possibility. In order to explore the creative structure of medical decision making, we must begin with this background awareness as it manifests in the milieu of the doctor-patient relationship. Then we can consider the creative steps whereby the objects of medical science come into being in the mind in responseto this background awareness.

Possibility as fundamental

The notion of possibility connects the mystical experience with the natural sciences. The actualization of possibility is the origin and purpose objective science.All objective formulation in the natural sciences emerges to grasp possibility as object for the subject, for the sake of the resulting subject-object interaction whereby possibility is actualized.

Thus, perception of possibility is the beginning andthe ultimate end of the scientific process in general, and of medical decision making in particular.

Normally when one speaks of "perception," one means intention toward an object. In fact, this was said to be the distinguishing feature of consciousness that setsit off from objective reality in mind, according to the early 20th-century philosopher Franz Brentano.

Our use of the word "perception" however is pre-objective. It refers to the domain in which the knowing subject senses herself to exist prior to the formulation of an objective world apart from the subject. Therefore, we occasionally will refer to direct "apprehension" of the domain of possibility, rather than to "perception" of possibility.

The first encounter with possibility in medicine

The young medical student, emerging from years of subdued classroom study and rote memorization of the medical sciences, such as anatomy, physiology and pharmacology, eventually is thrust into the theater of the emergency room.

Here he will encounter the sounds of human suffering, the smell of fresh blood and urine, the sharp tinkling of metal instruments on glass, and the barked orders and empathetic entreaties of medical caregivers.

His senses thereby are thrown into disarray, and his overriding impression simply that things are not as they should be. For him this is a horizon of open-ended human possibility, without form and void, with no organizing principle except for his new and daunting responsibility for its actualization.

Therefore, it is with great relief that he sees his attending physician enter the emergency suite. He calls out to him, "Hello, Professor Hippocrates!" The year is 400 BC.

Over the course of his career, this young clinician will recollect, with some anxiety, this initial encounter with an unstructured ground of possibility. It has initiated him and will help him to remain mindful of the source and ultimate charge of his professional role. It will give him courage to return to this unstructured ground in the milieu of the doctor-patient relationship.

Grasping possibility with metaphor

Imagine now, sometime later, in the year 1650 AD, when medical knowledge has progressed beyond the simple notion of the "balance of bodily humors" as in the time of Hippocrates.

The attending physician might direct the student to the bedside of a woman who is suffering from swollen legs. The student will come to this patient without a framework with which to understand the source of her suffering or how he might engage with it.

The attending physician, using the Socratic method of teaching, will introduce to the student a metaphor in terms of which to grasp this human possibility as an object for consideration, and with the theoretical toolsfor his intervention.

This chosen metaphor will be introduced surreptitiously, in the form of a question posed to the student regarding the clinical possibility before him.

For instance, the attending might ask the student, "If the heart is a pump that carries blood from the legs to therest of the body, what would you say about the conditionof this woman's heart?" As if responding to Socrates, the student must answer this question by using the same terms within which it was asked, thereby taking on this metaphor as a cognitive means of grasping the human possibility inherent in the clinical situation.

So the student might respond to his attending, "The heart pump appears to be failing, possibly due to a weak muscle wall, or maybe due to contracting too fast or slowly, or due to some physical obstruction." Thereby the student learns to explore and engage the phenomenon in front of him in terms of the hydrodynamic parameters of a pump.

The resulting object will appear to the student not asa metaphorical grasp of possibility, but as the grasped possibility itself. It will appear to be given as such. Thereby the student's devotion to perceived possibility is transferred to the created object as if it were the intendedend in itself.

Through the Socratic method, the pump metaphor will become for the student a "condition of the existence of the organism," as Nietzsche put it.

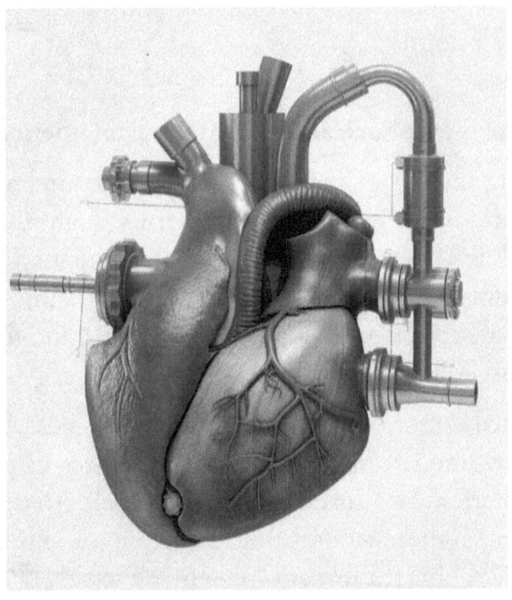

Heart as Pump. *Susan Saandholland on Midjourney*

This choice of the "pump" metaphor was not given. It had been introduced as a theory of heart function only in 1628 by Dr. William Harvey. So, for this student it was up-to-date medical science. But it was not the only metaphor proposed at that time with which to understand the circulatory role of the heart. Rene Descartes had disagreed with the "pump" model, preferring instead the notion of the heart as a "heating chamber" whereby circulation is affected.

It is not the choice of metaphor that matters, but its utility in the clinical situation. Through metaphor the student grasps possibility perceived in the patient. This is the beginning and the end of the medical decision. From the categories of the chosen metaphor are derived the objective data, the terms of measurement, and the points of causation with which to grasp possibility for is actualization.

The metaphorical fabric of medical science

The history of medical science is documented in the fabric of its metaphor-laden terms, such as "heart pump" or "hormonal axis" or "histocompatibility" or "neuralpropagation," or the "coded information" of the DNA of molecular biology. These are fluid and form to serve an end beyond themselves.

Furthermore, the application of metaphor evolves to accommodate not just specific instances of patient presentation, but the creative process itself. An example of this is the metaphorical structure of molecular biology, taking the form of "phenotype versus genotype" in our currently emerging paradigm shift.

The "phenotype" is a purely open-ended construct. It permits the creative grasp of possibility by any metaphor that achieves this end, such as eye color, body habitus, voice texture, hair pattern, personality type, intelligence, gender, race, cancer risk, even consciousness itself - each construed as an individual "trait."

The potential of this list is unlimited, as it serves to accommodate the open-ended perspective of the subject in response to the domain of human possibility. Thereby it renders an expansive power and creative liberty to the paradigm of molecular biology.

The "genotype," on the other hand, does not permit alternative metaphors of the subject's choosing. Instead, its utility is conferred by the singular root metaphor of "interactive molecules." The genotype construct takes the form of molecules proceeding from a dedicated genetic locus, and whose eventual interactions are said tocausally produce the phenotype.

Thereby, the genotype serves to render the final formulation in anthropic form, so that the intended possibility can be "grasped" as object for the subject, in the form of molecular interaction. In this way the genotype and phenotype serve their respective roles for acommon end.

The formulation of the molecular construct begins by positing the existence of, then searching for, a genetic locus that is named after the defined phenotype. This ad hoc process is similar to Hippocrates positing, then searching for, a "humoral imbalance" to explain a particular illness. In molecular biology this sets in motion the creative act of grasping possibility in terms of interacting molecules.

The unity of the art and the science of medicine

The creative grasp of human possibility will appear to the clinician as an act of objective "discovery." This singular act, seen from these two different perspectives, the creative and the objective, is where the "art" and the "science" of medicine come together.

Though the medical decision will appear to the clinician as an act of pure discovery, she will have a sense of a creative contribution from her own mind. We will describe this creative contribution in detail below, and why it must remain invisible to the clinician.

In analyzing the medical decision, we can see that, as stated by Eddington, the scientist is an "artist in disguise." [33] In medical science, as in physics, "the symbolic nature of the entities of physics is generally recognized; and the scheme of physics is now formulated in such a way as to make it almost self- evident that it is a partial aspect of something wider."[6]

This wider agenda in medicine is the grasp of humanpossibility for the sake of its actualization.

Looked at more broadly, we notice that "health and illness" are defined by each era in terms of the cosmology of that era, as cosmology serves to assert what counts as the basic elements of reality. By grasping human possibility in the negative as "illness," in terms of the cosmology of the era, the mind is directed toward its actualization as "health," taking these same terms as the tools of actualization.

At this higher level of abstraction, we see that the terms of "health versus illness" persist as a myth for medicine, to facilitate the creative application of the metaphors that comprise the cosmological terms of each era. Thereby a continuous lineage of medicine can persist, in terms of "health versus illness," despite the passing of discontinuous cosmologies over time. Underneath this metaphorical pastiche, there persists the unifying apprehension of possibility that is the milieu of the doctor-patient relationship.

The basic structure of the argument

In Chapter II, Possibility Theory, we will explore perception of possibility as the milieu of the doctor-patient relationship.

In Chapter III, Metaphor Induction, we will explore the creative process whereby metaphor is projected onto possibility, to grasp it as object for the subject in mind, and thereby to precipitate the subject-object interaction whereby possibility is actualized.

In Chapter IV, The Discovery Myth, we will explore how the language of scientific "discovery" has evolved as a myth to facilitate the creative process of metaphor induction.

In Chapter V, A Metadata Model, we will describe how possibility theory and metaphor induction differ from artificial intelligence, and outline a computer data model for decision-making based on possibility theory and metaphor induction. Therein we will illustrate the philosophical concepts we have described above as they pertain to the creative aspect of medical decision making and the social agenda of medicine, that we have herein called the "medical ethic."

Appendix A, at the end, is an optional review of the philosophical notions developed above, into a single unified argument.

CHAPTER II:
POSSIBILITY THEORY

"The greatest good is the knowledge of the union that themind has with the whole of nature."

- Spinoza

Possibility as fundamental

Perception of possibility is the fundamental level ofconsciousness. It is the mode in which the cosmos firstis aware of itself through the agency of the evolved brain. This manifests as individual consciousness and it takes the form of a knowable world set apart from a knowing subject in the brain-constituted theater of the mind. What we call "perception of possibility" is the universe's awareness of its own nature, deeper than actuality, but upon which all of actuality is based.

Perception of possibility is a mundane, yet primal, feature of all modes of cognition, whether scientific, aesthetic, moral, social, or contemplative. All that is "actual" partakes in possibility, for everything actual must be possible. But possibility is perceived as elemental and ontologically distinct from actuality.

When we state that a thing is possible, we insinuate possibility as a domain upon which actuality depends. When we argue that a premise might be true because it is possible, or that a premise cannot be true because it is not possible, we implicate awareness of possibility as a condition of truth.

Possibility is the mode in which the pre-objective laws of nature exist and give rise to actuality. Possibility renders ontological status to the probabilities that are represented by the fields of quantum theory. It manifests in the incidental actualities of life, such as the vertical orientation of tree trunks or the weight-bearing legs of Earth-dwellers as they implicate gravity. Possibility manifests as the variety of all life forms that arise through evolution. Evolution essentially is the emergence of possibility into actuality.

Perceiver and Perceived. *Susan Saandholland on Midjourney*

Possibility is the domain to which we respond when moved to affirm the truth of the Beatitudes of Jesus in the sermon on the mount, regardless of religious predilection. The mind recognizes possibility in these proclamations and feels compelled to defend their truth on this count. The meek have not inherited the earth, the merciful have not obtained mercy. But the meek have a moral claim to the earth in our hearts, and the merciful, in their mercy, affirm its reality. The use of the future tense in these terms situates their truth in the domain of possibility, even if they forever reside only there.

We perceive possibility as transcendental to time. It encompasses all that we call past, present and future. We easily acknowledge the reality of the "present" because it is experienced as actuality. We similarly attribute the reality of the past and of the future to the ground of possibility that they share with the present. We give names such as "eternity" (or the ancient Chinese term "history") to this domain of possibility in its entirety, thereby referring to its transcendental nature relative to all modes of time. As Plato said, "time is a moving image of eternity." [19]

Fritjof Capra pointed out in his helpful comparison of Eastern mysticism and modern physics that we have to go beyond the concepts of simple "existence and non- existence" when dealing with the domain of reality. [20] This is because its foundation lies in the possibility that is inherent in the void of space.

If one resists the notion of possibility as fundamental, if one maintains that only the "actual" is real, such that non-actuality is "nothing," then the domain of possibility can seem like an abyss of nothingness. In that case, one fails to recognize possibility as a horizon of creative potential. In the new physics, as Capra pointed out, the "physical vacuum" of field theory does not refer to mere nothingness, but contains the potential for an infinitevariety of physical forms. [22]

The milieu of the doctor-patient relationship

The milieu of the doctor-patient relationship is direct apprehension of human possibility, prior to the objectifying activity of the brain. The physician and the patient share in this broader domain of possibility.

This manifests as empathy. That is, empathy is more than just perception of possibility in the other. It is perception of the domain of possibility as the common ground of perceiver and perceived.

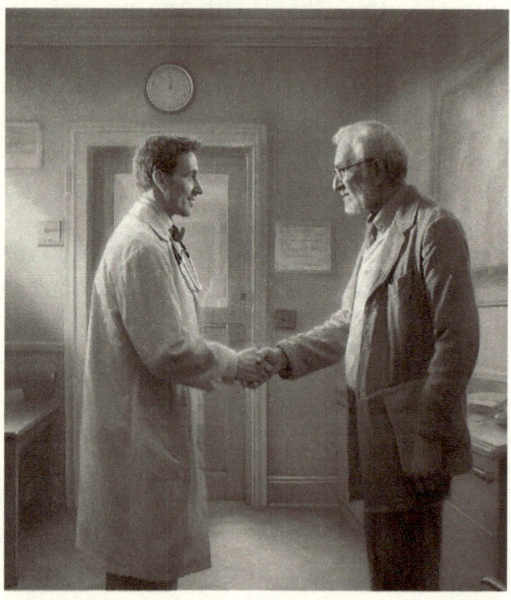

Doctor-Patient. *Susan Saandholland on Midjourney*

In the era of the physical sciences prior to relativity theory, conscious awareness was predicated upon the notion of an absolute separation of the observed world from the subjective observer. Thus, the goal of science was presumed simply to be the discovery of an intended object. This interactive dichotomy of subject and object was codified in the Cartesian duality.

Unfortunately, this dichotomy preempts an analysis of the common ground of possibility in which both the subject and object partake, including the doctor and patient. Therefore, it begins by obscuring the creative ground of the medical decision.

The genius of relativity theory was its collapse of the subject and the object back into their common domain. As Eddington said, the goal of relativity theory was no longer to separate the observer and the external world, but to recognize that in "our scientific description of natural phenomena, the two factors are indissolubly united." [14]

A return to the perspective of a common ground helps us to know where to begin in our analysis of the creative potential of medical decision making.

The creative imperative in medicine

As the clinician matures, her ability to recognize and to respond creatively to changing clinical situations should gradually improve.

Even in the early days of practice, this skill is essential and will be tested. The young doctor will encounter situations that require formulation of new therapeutic ends for her patient, ends that were not anticipated in her initial impression and its objective formulation.

The more challenging situations often will be

those that involve terminal illness, such as cancer, or kidney failure, or end-stage emphysema, or advanced dementia.

Initially the young physician might presume that the goal of treatment is simply the "prolongation of life," for this seems surely to be the natural agenda of the living. With this expectation, the young doctor will approach the clinical situation with her medical tools prepared to support this presumed end. Thus, she might choose among life-saving modalities, such as chemotherapy for cancer, or hemodialysis for kidney failure, or mechanical ventilation after a severe stroke, or a feeding tube for advanced dementia. She will have learned the statistical efficacy of each of these life-saving interventions, so that they become part of an evidence-based plan.

This plan will appear complete by virtue of its mere objectivity and the logical coherence with which it is formulated. Within the terms of the formulation, it will appear to entail the entire scope of the diagnostic and treatment options. Its logical necessity will appear as the "necessary truth" of the formulation itself. The young doctor will see no reason to doubt the correctness of the charted path. Her cognitive work will appear to be done.

Then doubt will arise. The patient or family might report a dissatisfaction with the treatment as it has been proposed. They might be troubled by the patient's persisting pain or dysfunction, or dependence upon others, such as the risk of becoming a burden that is inconsistent with the patient's resources or self-image.

The family, speaking on the patient's behalf, might report that she "would not want to continue this way." In the end, the patient or her family might simply say that "it is not worth it."

In this proclamation there manifests a subjective impression that has yet to take on an objective form. An unnamed feature of life is making itself known as more important than the presumed goal of the "prolongation oflife." At this point only a cry for help takes form.

That is, something remains undone that has yet tobe put into words. The initial impression exists only as an apprehension of unmet possibility. As of yet, there exist no terms whereby this perceived possibility can be grasped as an object for therapeutic intention.

The creative response to possibility

Situations like this require a creative initiative by the physician (or by the patient or family), to grasp the unaddressed possibility in objective form, so that it can be intended as a therapeutic goal.

For instance, the young doctor might envision a new goal of "quality of life" that supplants, and is superior to, the mere "prolongation of life."

The conditions of a quality life will differ among patients. For one patient it might mean, in fact, the prolonging of life at all costs. For another it might mean focusing on comfort or some other value at the expense of the length of life – goals such as living only while cognitive function remains good, or only long enough to say goodbye to a friend or family, or to witness some significant event such as the birth of a grandchild.

As Simeon, in the Nunc dimittis canticle of the 4th century, is made to say when finally seeing the newly born Jesus - and as captured in Rembrandt's painting "Simeon in the Temple" - "Now, Lord, you can let me, your servant, die in peace." Or as in Bach's aria, "I have had enough," we see the persuasion that quality life is more than mere prolongation.

The newly defined goal of "quality of life" might mean letting an intervening pathologic process proceed, such as an infection or progressive anemia, even if death is hastened thereby, if in so doing it permits a death with dignity.

Toward this end, the patient or family might decline antibiotics, or blood transfusion, or a feeding tube, or IV hydration, or other life-prolonging procedures, such as chemotherapy, or hemodialysis or surgery. A family might request withdrawal of a treatment already begun, such as mechanical ventilation or a feeding tube, feeling that it is "futile" in light of the newly defined goal.

In these changes the young doctor will discover that the medical decision requires a receptive posture in response to newly manifesting human possibility, as it is apprehended directly in the doctor-patient relationship.

The physician will come to understand that the derived "evidence-based" formulation relies upon this subjective impression, and that it manifests itself therein as an intermediate step, not as the end in itself.

The creative foundation of medical science

Today, in the parlors of the natural sciences, one increasingly speaks freely of the role of the observer in physics, of the anthropic elements of the objects of knowledge, of the selective influence of the instruments of measurement, of the incomplete and thus synthetic nature of mathematics, of the metaphorical components of theory, of a shifting of paradigms based on evolving cosmological theory and social myth.

This awareness of the perspectival and synthetic features of natural science has been slow to develop in medicine. Nevertheless, a nod to this impression was made by Light and Pillemer in their study of medical research, in which they concluded that the hope of removing all of subjectivity from statistical synthesis "seems not only ill-advised but impossible." [8]

Similarly, Matthew Cobb, in his modern history of molecular biology, describes a recent attempt to reduce genetics theory to pure information theory in light of the code-containing feature of DNA. He relates that this effort was frustrated by the fact that a strictly mathematical formula is devoid of the substance that is rendered by conceptual frameworks made of "words, metaphors and analogies." [7]

These metaphorical elements are what turn molecular biology into a tool for grasping human possibility, an end beyond mere information theory.

Despite such movement, there remains in medicine a deference to rigorous scientific objectivity, emerging during the 20th century as "evidence-based medicine." This well-intentioned notion is a throwback to a more naive time in science, when good science was felt to be devoid of subjective influence.

This was prior to relativity and quantum theory that recognize the anthropic elements in objective theory, and the limitative theorems in mathematics that acknowledge the synthetic nature of mathematical proof, and to the anthropological historiography of science in the works of Ernst Cassirer, Thomas Kuhn, Stephen Pepper, Stephen Toulmin, and others, in which cosmological and social paradigms are recognized as providing elemental notions for scientific discovery.

It is true that "evidence-based" rigor has rendered to medicine the benefits of modern science, such as coherence, testability, reproducibility, standardization and statistical certainty, as well as freedom from the tyranny of historical and institutional authority.

But a blind devotion to objectivity has resulted in medicine's failure to keep up with the evolution in science that seeks to understand the role of its own creative hand in objective theory. Medicine is left unable clearly to account for how its objective formulations emerge in response to, and thus to serve, a deeper humanistic agenda. An artifact of this limitation is that the relationship between the art and the science of medicine remains obscure.

The need for this understanding is more urgent in medicine than in other areas of science. Medicine must engage objective knowledge in the service of subjective impression, specifically with regard to human suffering, and often with regard to the encounter with death and its meaning in the human agenda. Posing these questions is necessary if one is to do full justice to the nature and charge of the doctor-patient relationship.

The metaphorical grasp of possibility

In our example of end-of-life care above, there was nothing to dictate the choice of the metaphor "quality of life" to grasp the human possibility manifesting in the emerging patient situation. The choice of this metaphor was discretional. This metaphor was selected because it accommodated the sense and range of the worth of life regardless of length of life. Any number of metaphors might have served this same end.

This underscores the fact that the goal of medicine is not to find the "correct" metaphor, but to select a metaphor that effectively grasps human possibility. As Eddington said of the new physics, "It was found that science could accomplish so much with entities whose nature was left in suspense that it began to be questioned whether there was any advantage in removing the suspense." [15]

The decision to choose a metaphor, and thereby to grasp some aspect of possibility as an intended object, is driven by the intention to actualize perceived possibility. Its success or failure in the end is evaluated based on this same measure. The specific metaphor chosen for this end is a function of the perspective of the user. The evaluation of a treatment plan as "worth it" can be made only by the patient or other vested party. It necessarily is a subjective impression.

On this count, our example of the quality-of-life metaphor is an imperfect illustration of the creative application of metaphor to grasp human possibility as object. This is because the notion of "quality," as an intended object, still presumes a subjective impression, so that its subjective origin remains apparent. It is notyet an example of how purely objective terms, such as the "genetic locus" in molecular biology, arise from the application of metaphor.

We began with "quality of life" because it is a more transparent illustration of the creative application of metaphor in response to perceived possibility. We have yet to show that every objective formulation in medical science, including those that appear devoid of subjective impression, such as molecular biology, arise from a creative response to subjective apprehension of human possibility. This will come later.

The Socratic method

In the last chapter we reviewed an instance of the application of metaphor manifesting as the Socratic method in medical education. In that case, the teacher asked the student a question about his patient's heart in terms of its function as a "pump."

Thereby the pump as metaphor was projected onto the clinical possibility. It became the way in which the student engaged heart failure in her patient, by providing the cognitive tools with which clinical possibility was grasped and actualized.

We can learn more about the basic features of metaphor application by observing the Socratic method as it manifests in the dialogues of Plato. For instance, in Plato's dialogue, The Sophist, Plato explores his impression of those hired teachers of wisdom in his day called "sophists." His impression of the sophist is grasped in objective terms by applying the root metaphor"angler" (fisherman).

In terms of this "angler" metaphor, Socrates states that the sophist and the angler each appears to be a hunter, "one going to the seashores... while the othergoes to waters of another sort - rivers of wealth." [77]

In this formulation Plato is not proposing that the "angler" is a metaphorical grasp of possibility inherent inthe sophist. He is proposing that the sophist simply is an angler. To his audience the sophist appears discovered to be an angler. That is, the object does not appear as a metaphorical grasp of possibility, but as the grasped possibility itself. In this way, devotion to possibility is transferred to the object as the end in itself.

Sophist as Angler. *Susan Saandholland on Midjourney*

We note also that this objective formulation of the sophist as an "angler" takes on a logical coherence, as Socrates describes features of the sophist in terms of the categories of the angler. Thereby, the resulting construct assumes the form of a logical proof because the applied categories appear to lead back to the angler root metaphor, from which they were derived, as their necessary conclusion. For instance, in that the sophist is found to be a "hunter for tame animals at rivers of wealth," he appears necessarily to be an angler.

In this way, the "logical necessity" emerging from the metaphorical coherence appears as the "necessary truth" of the formulation itself. It appears given.

But there are many other metaphors that Plato might have chosen with which to define the sophist. The choice of "angler" accommodated Socrates' impression of the sophist as an opportunist. It thereby reflects his perspective and his trajectory of intention regarding the possibility perceived in the sophist.

Metaphor application in medical education

Similarly, the role of classroom medical education is to arm the young doctor with metaphorical constructs that she will use to grasp the horizon of human possibility that she will encounter in the clinic.

For instance, the medical student might be introduced in her pharmacology course to the notion of drugs as "transmitters of chemically-coded information." From a study guide distributed in our medical pharmacology class some years ago one reads...

"Drugs represent 'chemically coded information.'

The effect of most drugs is the result of their interaction with macromolecular components of cells. Note that the macromolecular components are the 'receptors.' There are two different kinds of receptors: a) 'Drug receptors' - molecules in the cell for some other reason but which bind the drug; b) 'receptors for endogenous regulatory ligands' - molecules which normally act as receptors. They have two distinct functions: 1) a 'binding' function, and 2) an 'effector/action' domain."

In this excerpt, the chosen root metaphor is "coded information." It provides the sub-categories in terms of which the finer details of clinical possibility are grasped - categories such as "regulatory ligands" or "binding function" or "action domain." In this way, a logically- coherent construct emerges, in terms of the categories of the applied root metaphor of "coded information."

Using the Socratic method of teaching, an attending physician might ask a medical student a leading question in terms of this "coded-information" root metaphor.

For instance, regarding the administration of digoxin to a patient with heart failure, the attending physician might ask a student, "What chemically-coded message does digoxin deliver to the muscles of the heart to make it pump better?" This question requires the student to conceive of the action of this drug in terms of delivered "chemically-coded information." It thereby provides the metaphorical causality with which to grasp and actualize the intended possibility.

To this student, the terms of "chemically-coded

information" will not appear as a metaphorical grasp of clinical possibility. They will appear as the grasped possibilities themselves. They will appear given as the products of objective discovery.

A critically-thinking medical student might object to the terms of the posed question. For instance, she might protest that she was taught by her favorite pharmacologyprofessor that drugs are in fact "keys that unlock" inherent chemical processes, not "carriers of chemically-coded information."

This is ultimately a disagreement about the choice of metaphor, not about the goal of the medical decision. The goal is not to find the "right" metaphor. It is not even to avoid metaphor. Instead, the goal is to use metaphor for the grasp and actualization of human possibility as it is apprehended in the clinical situation.

Though the specific metaphor with which one grasps possibility is not given, the possibility that one apprehends is given to consciousness. The metaphor on the other hand is an existential choice, driven by the user's perspective with regard to the intended possibility,and the trajectory of intention regarding its actualization.

The creative use of the physical sciences

Medicine is practiced and taught in terms of the physical sciences. Thereby medicine appears essentially to be a project of the physical sciences. However, medicine is not itself a physical science. Rather, it essentially is a social science that uses the physical sciences creatively for its deeper humanistic agenda, thatis the actualization of human possibility.

The notion of a creative use of the physical sciences is counter-intuitive to the modern ear. This is because the physical sciences function by appearing as the ends- in-themselves in any project to which they are applied. So, for instance, when medicine is practiced as anatomy or physiology or pharmacology, it appears to be simply aproject and product of anatomy, physiology, or pharmacology.

But, as every healthcare worker knows, medicine ceases to be medicine if its tools are used for their objective ends only, rather than in the service of its deeper human calling. This agenda, revealed in our analysis of the structure of medical decision making, is the perception of human possibility for the sake of its actualization.

Despite this creative activity, the popular notion of medical decision making is that of a straight-forward logical proof, with necessary conclusions derived from given data and their inherent logical connections. This is formalized as "evidence-based medicine."

The evidence-based decision appears to emerge from rigorous observation alone, that is, as a passive act. There is no role in this conception for an active, creative initiative or synthetic response to a more deeplyperceived domain of possibility.

The medical decision as a creative response

The physicist David Bohm stressed that fundamental reality is an unbroken wholeness, an "inseparable quantum interconnectedness," that we artificially carve up as theoretical objects for our subjective need. [55] In possibility theory we have proposed a way to refer to this background wholeness as direct apprehension of the domain of possibility.

The medical decision emerges as a creative response to this domain of possibility in the milieu of the doctor-patient relationship. This subjective act determines what will count as clinical data, and the terms of measurementand intervention. It is not a passive act.

For example, consider a patient with Alzheimer-type dementia, who can be expected to manifest progressive decline in cognitive function over time. At each point in his follow-up visits this change will warrant a modification of the treatment plan, driven by his subjective needs relative to his decline.

The need for comfort and dignity, though always present, will take different forms over his course. His requirements for physical and intellectual stimulation, though always present, will evolve. This will influence the kind and the timing of medicines and other arrangements, such as the location and structure of his supportive environment, and the prognosis that is given to the family.

The mere anatomic and physiologic changes in the brain of the patient with Alzheimer's dementia, in isolation from their subjective meaning, will render no effective clinical decision points for the family. These objective changes "become disease" only by virtue of their subjective meaning to the patient and family.

The anthropic conditions of knowing

The terms that emerge to grasp human possibility do not arise only from our trajectory of intention regarding the patient. They are formed also by the need to grasp possibility as an object for the subject. That is, the object must take on anthropic characteristics.

An example of this is the notion in molecular biology of "histo-compatibility." In the mid-20th century, based on experiments with tumors transplanted into mice, a set of proteins on cell surfaces was found to be associated with immunologic rejection of the transplanted cancer cells. Therefore, these cell-surface proteins were called "histo-compatibility" proteins, reflecting their phenotypically-conceived function.

The formulation of a genetic origin for these proteins began by positing the existence of a histo-compatibility "locus" in the genome, where these proteins are encoded. Eventually this genetic locus was found to reside on chromosome six.

The notion of tissue compatibility is transparently anthropic. It derives historically from the narrow focusof these initial laboratory experiments.

Genes do not come with such names assigned to them. The metaphorical origin of the name is the contribution of the mind to the formed object. It reflects human possibility as it is perceived by the clinician. Just as in the case of Socrates' definition of the sophist as an "angler," it represents a trajectory of intention regarding human possibility, providing the manner in which clinical data are defined, measured and causally connected in theory.

This is not to say that genetic loci "do not exist." It is to say that their existence, as loci, is a function of the user's anthropic perspective, for the purpose of the subject-object interaction whereby human possibility is grasped and actualized.

Nevertheless, this histo-compatibility locus and its products will appear to the clinician not as a metaphorical grasp of possibility, but as the grasped possibility itself. Nature will appear to have provided a "histo-compatibility" locus that we merely appropriate.

The anthropic nature of these terms persists in the metaphorical categories with which finer details of the intended human possibility are grasped. So, for instance, in treating a viral infection, the clinician may conceive of a patient's white blood cells as "recognizing a virus as foreign." As a medical text says, one anticipates finding "signaling" molecules, called cytokines, helping branches of the immune system to "talk to each other and respond to threats." [84]

The formulation thereby emerges with a coherence in terms of the categories of "tissue compatibility," and within the broader metaphorical context of the "interactive molecules" of molecular biology.

Subjective versus objective knowledge

The nature of medical decision-making is of singular interest to intellectual history because of this interdependence of subjective and objective thought. This question of the nature of the interdependence of objective and subjective knowing, and its meaning for the human enterprise, is central to intellectual history.

This manifests, for instance, as questions of faith versus reason, of the social and ethical consequences of material reductionism and mechanization, of the natural evolution of consciousness and the source of its value judgments, of the ontological status of mathematics, of the notion of the divine in a material world, even of democracy and individual freedom. For all these things, the creative origins of objective thought in medicine can be a paradigm.

Let us pause briefly therefore to clarify what we mean by subjective versus objective knowledge.

By subjective knowledge we mean the non-reflective familiarity fostered through association with phenomena. By objective knowledge, on the other hand, we mean the data and their logical relations that emerge from metaphor-laden theories that are applied to thissubjective impression.

A simple illustration is our knowledge of Aunt Bessie. By "subjective impression" we mean the way in which one knows Aunt Bessie personally, such as familiarity with her face, her voice, her gait as seen froma distance, and her personal predilections, and so thekind of interaction that one anticipates having with her when she arrives at the airport tomorrow for a visit.

This subjective knowledge of Aunt Bessie is non-reflective. It does not require reduction to data or measurement. Nevertheless, such knowledge is a deep well of reserve that characterizes all areas of human cognition of any consequence. Even when knowledge is reduced to data for specific purposes, it originates from this well of familiarity. This corresponds to the direct apprehension of possibility that characterizes the milieu of the doctor-patient relationship.

Conversely, by "objective knowledge" of Aunt Bessie we mean a description of her that might be given to someone who has never met her, but who must recognize her to pick her up tomorrow from the airport.

Unlike the familiarity of subjective impression, this objective knowledge of Aunt Bessie is theory-laden. It is characterized by a reduction to data and their explicit logical relations as derived from terms of theory, such as body habitus or hair color or personality type, that give structure to what is experienced. This corresponds to evidence-based decision making in medicine.

This objective knowledge empowers action. It provides the terms of causality and tools of actualization. It makes it possible for one to "find" Aunt Bessie, even if one never has met her. For this reason, objective knowledge is the more auspicious form of knowledge. It often is referred to as knowledge itself because of its venerated status.

Objective knowledge is limited by the boundaries of the metaphors upon which its theories and data are based. It does not manifest as a deep source as does subjective knowledge in response to perception of open- ended possibility.

If one identifies Aunt Bessie from a distance based purely on objective knowledge, this must be an act of cognition different in character from the recognition of Aunt Bessie by a person who knows her. And it does not have the capacity to self-correct on its own terms, for instance if one brings home the wrong person from the airport.

Taking this as our distinction between subjective and objective knowledge, we note that every area of intellectual activity involves both subjective and objective elements, comingled in peculiar ways that reflect the needs of each domain of cognitive activity. Every cognitive enterprise renders more or less weight to one element or to the other. So, for instance, in the arts or in psychology one renders more weight to subjective impression, whereas in architecture or in physics, one gives preference to the objective form of thought.

But this relative weight is notoriously not the case in medicine. In medicine, there is no preferential weight given to the subjective or the objective form of thought.

Instead, the subjective and the objective elements act with equal weight and in equal deference to each other.

For instance, a patient who presents to her doctor with rheumatoid arthritis might be found to have certain objective findings, such as a measurable degree of tissue inflammation that is determined by lab measurement, or of boney joint degeneration that is apparent on x-ray. But the significance of these objective measurements, the feature that makes them "disease," is their subjective meaning for the patient.

Objective changes in lab results or x-ray findings on their own have no meaning or relevance to the medical decision without this subjective impression. The human body is replete with variations from the norm that do not rise to the designation of "disease," just because of the absence of this subjective determinant.

This subjective input is communicated in terms of the patient's "symptoms," such as joint pain, or in terms of relevance to her life, such as how her symptoms affect performance at work or her ability to care for herself or to make life plans. The clinician never can turn away from this well of subjective knowledge, to a consideration of objective measurements in isolation, because symptoms, as the well of direct apprehension of human possibility, are the elements that give meaning to objective changes as "disease."

Objective data themselves are limited by the metaphorical boundaries of the theory from which they are derived. Subjective input from the patient often will require more from the physician than these finite parameters permit.

But the doctor also cannot turn away from objective knowledge, and to subjective impression in isolation. For only with these objective terms can the clinician "do something" for the patient.

That is, only through the resulting subject-object interaction can the possibility perceived in the doctor- patient relationship be actualized.

So, the physician must learn to accommodate both of these sources of knowledge, and at the same time. Reading objective test results must be accompanied by empathy for the patient. The doctor must know rheumatoid arthritis in the way that one knows Aunt Bessie.

The hazard of data as ends in themselves

The codification of medical data has contributed to their appearance as ends in themselves in the decision-making process. Therein they have lost connection to thebroader cosmic domain that renders to them clinical meaning. An example of this is the ICD code set ("International Statistical Classification of Diseases"), that lists all currently-used diagnostic and treatment terms along with a distinguishing numerical code.

So, for instance, the diagnosis called "viral gastroenteritis" has the code A08, and the diagnosis called "dysentery" has the code A09. This codification, that has its origin as a tool of billing, assumes on an unwarranted role in clinical decision making.

Diagnoses come into being for the sake of the subject-object interaction whereby possibility is grasped and actualized. As objects for the subject, therefore, these metaphorical products must be free to evolve through engagement with possibility. But codification introduces stagnation into an object, as the numerical code cannot serve the same function as the metaphor. The resulting natural evolution of diagnostic terms is aborted if a diagnosis is treated as a codified end in itself.

For example, in the paradigm shift to molecular biology, one must be free to ask, regarding diabetes, what it "really is" in terms of molecular biology. This question does not occur if diabetes can be nothing but itself, codified as "E11." One is not free to de-construct the number, as one can a theoretical entity, in the serviceof a newly-emerging paradigm.

Similarly, the illness called "peptic ulcer disease" was once thought to be an endocrine disease, caused by over-production of stomach acid. It now is known to be an infectious disease in most cases, caused by the bacterium Helicobacter pylori that invades the bowel wall. What if the parameters of codification had confined peptic ulcer disease to a category of endocrine disease?

Similarly, it has been thought that the "neurologic" system of the body is physiologically isolated from the "immunologic" system. This is an artifact of their metaphorically-distinct formulations.

For example, it has seemed that rheumatoid arthritis, a disease of the immune system, has nothing to do with the nervous system. But it has been demonstrated that stimulation of the vagus nerve somehow centrally blocks inflammation in the spleen, the organ where the immunologic system is mediated.

To explore this anomaly fully, one must appreciate that the physiologic categories, as they are defined, are provisional. One must be free from the implied "given" nature of these categories, so that one might envision new physiologic categories that, if necessary, subsume what we now call the neurologic and the immunologic systems.

Consider the distinct but clinically similar diseases "viral gastroenteritis" and "bacterial dysentery," codified respectively as A08 and A09. Each is characterized by diarrhea, dehydration, fever, rash, and confusion. Imagine a medical student who is directed by her attending to evaluate an elderly woman in the emergencyroom who presents with the symptoms of diarrhea, dehydration, fever and confusion.

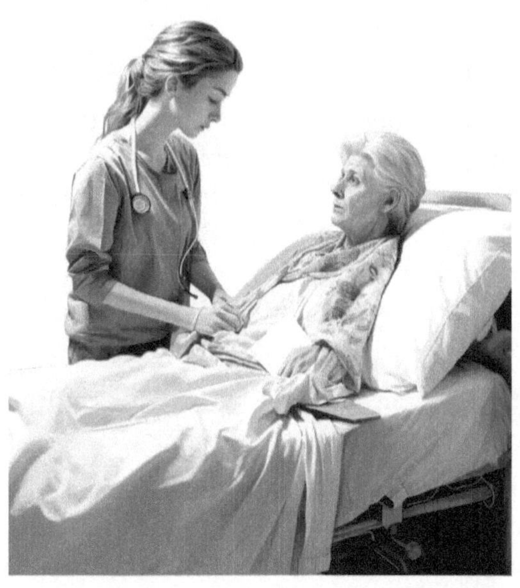

Bedside Exam. *Susan Saandholland on Midjourney*

After evaluating this patient, the student might turn toher computer for diagnostic assistance. There she might discover that the disorder of "viral gastroenteritis" presents as diarrhea, dehydration, fever and confusion. She returns to her attending physician to report that this elderly patient appears to have viral gastroenteritis and that she can be treated conservatively in the ED with IV hydration and returned to home with reassurance and to recover with bed rest.

The experienced attending, however, knows that symptoms such as "diarrhea, dehydration, fever and confusion" refer to a reality that is broader in scope of meaning than can be captured in the mere objectivity of their terms. Therefore, he accompanies the medical student back to the patient's room, where the full meaning of these findings can be explored and learned inthe milieu of the doctor-patient interaction.

Upon entering the patient's room, the attending physician pauses for a few seconds, then frowns. To confirm his suspicion, he approaches the patient's bedside. He says "Hello, Ms. Brown," and awaits her response. He then extends the tips of his fingers to touch her skin. With this, he shakes his head, and exits the room to discuss his impression with the student.

"Your patient does not have viral gastroenteritis," the attending says. "She has dysentery."

This distinction is important because, though dysentery presents, as does viral gastroenteritis, with diarrhea, dehydration, fever and confusion, it is a far more dangerous condition. This patient might die of sepsis or possibly of bowel perforation if treated only conservatively with IV fluids in the ED and sent home.

The embarrassed medical student might protest thatthe patient had "all of the objective findings" that the computer said were characteristic of viral gastroenteritis.In response, the attending will give these directions to the student: "When you walk into the room, smell thediarrhea. Take note of its peculiarly-toxic odor. This isnot characteristic of viral diarrhea. Feel the remarkable degree of heat arising from the patient's body as it fillsthe space around her. Look at the hew of her red-flushedskin, and note its whole-body distribution. You will notsee these things in viral gastroenteritis, at least not in this way."

"Finally," he will say, "note the nature of the patient's confusion. Ask yourself if she seems merely to be cognitively slowed due to malaise from fever and dehydration, or if she seems disoriented, out of proportion to what one might expect from these factors alone. Should one suspect instead a toxic effect on the brain, such as an encephalopathy arising from systemic products of a bacterial infection?"

The attending is therein asking the student to know these symptoms subjectively as she would know Aunt Bessie.

These considerations arise from approaching the patient from the perspective of the direct apprehension of possibility that gives meaning to the diagnostic terms. It ensures that in the future the student will "recognize" the peculiar smell, fever, and delirium of dysentery. She will be familiar with them because of this anecdotalencounter. They will carry a meaning for her that they cannot possess on their own as codified ends in themselves.

With this encounter, the student learns more than just the specific findings associated with dysentery. She learns that objective findings point to a deeper reality, that can be known only through the subjective encounter with possibility in the doctor-patient milieu.

She will develop a healthy suspicion of computer data appearing as ends in themselves. She will know that anecdotal knowledge is not just an inferior form of data- based knowledge, but a different kind of knowledge - a familiarity more substantive than mere data.

Possibility in quality management

Due to the hypnotic aspect of metaphor, data often are mistaken as the ends in themselves in the quality management process. That is, they are mistaken as the measure of quality itself, rather than as tools of quality practice.

A tool of quality and a measurement of quality are useful in the same clinical domain, but are different phenomena that serve different functions.

Consider for example the lab test called Hemoglobin A1c (H1c), that is a measure of the amount of glucose attached to a patient's red blood cells at any one time. Red blood cells live for three months after being born in the bone marrow. During their three-month life in the blood stream they collect glucose on their cell surface. Therefore, the H1c is a measurement of a patient's average blood glucose over any previous three months.

This measurement helps the clinician to know the effectiveness of treatment, and to guide the clinician in adjusting the patient's treatment, such as adjusting her daily insulin dose.

That is, this objective measurement of H1c is a tool of quality medical decision-making. However, if the H1c is treated as an end in itself, it can be mistaken as a direct measure of the quality of the medical decision.

For instance, one might assume that a medical practice whose diabetic patients all have a normal H1c must be practicing quality care. However, this result might reflect a decision by a medical group to discharge from their practice all those patients whose diabetes is difficult to manage, so that no poorly-controlled diabetic patients remain in their practice. If the H1c is indeed the end-in-itself, then one must concede that this medical practice manages diabetes well.

The problem with this approach is that diabetes mellitus is a "disease" not because of a high blood glucose, but because of the practical meaning of a high glucose to the life of the patient. For instance, diabetic patients suffer from complications such as neuropathy, immunodeficiency, vascular disease, kidney failure, heart failure, and blindness.

It is management of diabetes at this level, at the level of its complications and their subjective meaning to the patient, that determines quality care. The H1c is a tool toward that deeper end, not a measure of it.

The clinician might need to adjust a patient's insulin dose to address and avoid these complications. But he also might need to counsel the patient on a better diet. He might need to help her address life stressors or co-morbidities that impede glucose control. He might need to adjust the treatment plan or expectations of outcome to accommodate a patient's limited resources or social supports. He might need to be available to a "brittle" patient after hours to help avoid hospitalizations, or be supportive of a family struggling with anticipation of diabetes-related disability.

The medical decision begins and ends with this direct apprehension of open-ended possibility. Therefore, the management of the patient's illness is a creative enterprise. Quality of care is a function of this creative response. The H1c does not measure this creative response.

Indeed, a medical practice that cares for poor or brittle patients - whose blood glucose values are typically erratic - can expect, on average, relatively poor H1c results. But the quality of care of this practice, as a measure of addressing human need, is better than that of a practice that merely discharges their difficult patients. So, the H1c in this case might be inversely related to the quality of care, rather than a direct measure of it.

The health care manager who merely tracks H1c asan end in itself will mistake it as a measure of quality. It is better to have a system designed to support quality decision making by rendering the H1c measurement available to the practitioner as a tool of quality decision-making.

Computer decision-making

In all thought there is an element deeper than the physical objects of awareness... there is awareness itself.

We call this consciousness. In 1974 Thomas Nagel wrote a now-classic essay titled "What is it like to be a bat?" [69] The importance of this essay for our purpose is the question that it begs: that it is "like something" to be a bat, that is, that there is a distinct phenomenon called conscious.

.

Conscious Bat. *Susan Saandholland on Midjourney*

We believe that the bat has consciousness becausethe bat behaves as though it is interacting with the same domain of possibility that characterizes our awareness. Itresponds not simply to accommodate this domain, but asif aware of this domain.

The bat's apprehension of this domain might be qualitatively different from ours, reflecting a diverging path of evolution, but not a diverging source.

In light of this, the problem with the notion of communicating with a computer is that a computer is notconscious. Unlike the bat, it is not "like anything" to be a computer. The computer does not perceive a response to the domain of possibility in which it partakes.

As pointed out by the linguist, Noam Chomsky, there is nothing inherent to the algorithms and calculations of AI tools to distinguish their occasional erroneous output (designated by the anthropic term "hallucinations") from inherently truthful statements, other than the human artifacts that were scanned into them and that were at one time determined to be truthful within their own domain, a domain that now is static.

Unlike human calculations, that are a real-time response to a domain of possibility in which the subject partakes, the calculations of AI are a response to nothingexcept to these original scanned artifacts. These calculations render a coherence to the output; but they are not a guarantor of truth. Only were consciousness nothing but calculation could this be otherwise.

The plethora of anthropomorphic terms used to describe AI tends to blur the distinction between human creative response and machine calculation. The human action relies upon on the organic course-correcting source that is perception of possibility. The machine does not. The computer is not organically connected with the domain of possibility, as is the evolved brain. It is in no way an evolved manifestation of the universe knowing itself. Thus, there is no common ground for "communicating," and certainly not for communicating ashared reference.

Programming a computer to interact with a user as if the computer had consciousness, in what has come to be called "artificial intelligence," does not render a state of consciousness to the computer. It renders a simulation, so that the term "simulated intelligence" might be more appropriate.

As the computer is a tool for calculation, its substrate is called "information," managed in terms of bits. To believe that calculation reproduces consciousness requires mistaking information as fundamental to the universe apart from the perceiving subject. However, information, as information, exists only as an anthropic tool of the perceiver. It has no meaning, no existence as information, apart from the perceiving subject. It is how the subject grasps and talks about the more fundamental domain of possibility.

If the clinician turns her attention away from the patient, and toward the computer, then her connection with the domain of possibility that she shares with the patient is broken.

As a tool in the service of consciousness, a computer can create output that is meaningful for a conscious agent. That is, the notion of "interacting with a computer" is meaningful if it is used in concert with the subject's own apprehension of possibility. This is a useful role for what is called artificial intelligence in the context of the doctor-patient relationship.

Aesthetics and AI

This is a good place to turn our attention to the roleof AI tools in art, as many of the themes that pertain to the creative features of medical decision making are played out in even more demonstrable fashion in the creative domain of art.

It is not surprising that AI can compose a poem

that will move us as does Wordsworth, or generate a digital work of art that imitates the techniques of Rubens or Rembrandt. In fact, it would be surprising if it could not. It is not surprising then that the artist and poet might perceive this as an existential threat. Clarifying the nature of AI, and its natural limitations, can be helpful inameliorating this threat.

In the same way that the Deep Blue computer program was created in 1989 to "win" against a world-class chess champion by anticipating all possible chess moves, the tools of AI in art and prose are created by sampling all available human artifacts in their respective domains, then recursively creating computational routines to arrive at the demonstrably desired ends by the most exacting means possible.

These "desired ends" in AI are derived from the already-established ends, explicit or implicit, discovered upon sampling, such as the statistically-likely next word in a sentence string, or graphical features created by artists and manifesting through recursive comparison with existing documents.

But these are not the same "desired ends" of the artist who is creating a work of art de novo. For this artist, the creative urge is an artifact of consciousness. That is, it is driven by awareness, by direct apprehension of the vast domain of open-ended cosmic possibility, of which she herself is a manifestation, and that defines her role and cosmic significance.

Her task is not a dispassionate calculation toward a previously-determined end. It is a creative response to perception of this domain, to grasp it as an object for contemplation, in words, images and sounds that evoke joy, grief, awe, psychic confrontation and ultimately healing. In this way, she probes the universe for meaning and reconciliation. As the 20th century philosopher, Ernst Cassirer, said in his Philosophy of theEnlightenment...

The creation of the artist is no mere product of subjective imagination, no empty phantasm; it is an expression of true being in the sense of an inner necessity and law. Genius does not receive its law from without, but from within itself; it produces thislaw in its original form. And now it appears that this form which was not borrowed from nature is, nevertheless, in complete harmony with it, that it does not contradict the fundamental form of nature but rather discovers and confirms this form.

So, for instance, the poet Rilke, the artist van Gogh, the composer Handel, all were responding to what they conceived of as a sense of the "divine" - a domain separate from them, yet in interaction with which they sought meaning. As John Donne wrote in the 17th century these salient words that became the text of anaria in the 2005 opera, Atomic Doctor, as a petition tothe divine for guidance pertaining to nuclear war, "Battermy heart... for I, except you enthrall me, never shall be free."

AI can scour and sample such sources to computationally create similar works, even producing similar psychic effects for the listening patron. But AI cannot feel or understand what drove John Donne towrite these words, nor intuit how this relates to the theories of Marcus Aurelius 1500 years before in his Meditations on the formative role of suffering in human becoming. The tool of AI cannot know what it means to be racked with anxiety about a desire to reconcile with the universe.

This is because AI is not conscious. It does not have secondary qualia such as pain or the experience of color or of regret. It does not "feel" or "understand" or "relate" or "know" or have any "sense" of being right or of becoming what it has it in it to be. When we use these terms to refer to AI computations, we are anthropomorphizing their computational activity and output with terms drawn from our own experience; for

AI is programed to satisfy these human expectations in us - with the result that it simulates them, and appears to reproduce them. But, unlike a bat or Rembrandt, it is not "like anything" to be a computer or an AI computation. It cannot respond creatively to perception of a universe in which it partakes.

The popular notion that a machine can be "conscious" derives from a combination of two problematic notions of consciousness: the computational and the solipsistic. The "computation model" poses consciousness as nothing but logical management of information, that supposedly develops awareness merely with progressive complexity of computation. The second notion is that consciousness is generated entirely by the brain with no external input - that is, entirely "between the ears" -solipsistically sealed off from others and from the rest ofthe cosmos.

Combining these two notions, it is reasonable to assume that if the same matrix of calculations that occurs between the ears is made also to occur in a machine, despite a different electronic substrate, then consciousness emerges.

A very different model was imagined by Carl Sagan when he said that "we are a way for the cosmos to know itself," or when Alan Dressler observed that, through consciousness, "the Universe has invented a way to know itself," or when Thomas Nagel says that consciousness is the process of "the universe gradually waking up and becoming aware of itself."

That is, consciousness is not just awareness of the universe; it is the universe becoming aware, through the agency of the evolved brain. This is not speaking metaphorically, but mechanically. The brain is that organ evolved as the channel through which the universe comes to know itself as an objective world existing apartfrom a subjective knower in the theater of the mind. To create such a world, the brain must be able to perceive and engage the domain of cosmic possibility in which it partakes.

A computational AI machine cannot be "conscious" because, unlike the brain, it has not evolved as a manifestation of the universe whereby the universe knows itself. The brain might use "computation" (or be thought of as using computation) in its creative response. But the foundation of this creative response, its substance, is the ground of cosmic possibility in which itpartakes. This might be said to be a "channeling theory" of consciousness, to distinguish it from the "computational theory" of consciousness.

However, when a calculated work of AI creates in us a sense of awe, it is not because we are "fooled" by it. This inspirational response attests to our own connection to the universe and says nothing of the AI tool. Even a haphazard configuration of sand dunes blown by the wind can create an inspirational response in the right receiver. As Emerson pointed out, when we read the prose of a writer, our understanding comes from the voice of the universe through the writer, not from the writer, who is on this count superfluous.

If the mere ability to evoke a response warrants the designation of "art," then the calculated products of AI, no less than the artist's creative response, must be called "art." But if the artist's direct apprehension and intention to communicate the content of the universe is required for what we reserve as "art," then AI cannot be called art.

The concern is that the illusion resulting from simulation will grow until the non-discriminating mind resigns from the human project that is called art. One will quit asking "what is art?" We will forget how to value or recognize the role of the artist who responds creatively to the cosmos, to grasp it in terms that can speak to others. In giving up this process, we diminish our humanity. We settle instead for the mere pressing of a button whenever an evocative conceptual picture is needed.

By making clear these distinctions - that art requires a conscious agent, that AI is not conscious, that conscious awareness is not computation, that artificial intelligence, being computation, is simulated intelligence, that unlike AI the artist is a participant in the universe that she describes, that her work is a creative response to this cosmic domain, that her work is a necessary feature of the human dilemma - then we can be reassured that AI cannot replace the human need and reality of the artist.

The need for a new model of decision making

Current models of medical decision making often take the form, at their root, of algorithms that represent data as the given elements of the decision, and their logical coherence as their inherent structure. From this, a decision tree is constructed that shows all possible decision points and their probable outcomes. One presumes that a computer tool based on such an algorithm, in that it contains the essential elements of the medical decision, is able to make the decision in lieu of, or on behalf of, the clinician.

It is true that an algorithmic decision-tree can serve as a useful prop for the decision-maker. It can make explicit the elements of the clinician's creative response to possibility. But this objective structure contains no representation of the creative process itself whereby such a decision tree comes into being. Therefore, such a model will not do as a tool for medical decision making, for it is missing the creative element.

Without this creative interface, a computer tool will impede the decision-making process. It will force the clinician to turn away from the lived possibility as it is perceived in the patient, so to accommodate the static elements of the algorithm, to defer to them.

It is true that the mature clinician will come to anticipate that every objective formulation, such as a diagnosis or treatment plan, is provisional by its very nature. That is, the formulation is temporary, not because it is imperfect, but because it exists to serve an end beyond itself. Still, the clinician will be tempted to defer to objectivity, as represented in the decision tree, as if it contains the sufficient conditions of the medical decision.

To counteract this temptation, it was sufficient in the early 20th century for Dr. Francis Peabody to say to the class of Harvard medical students that "the secret of the care of the patient is in caring for the patient." In Peabody's time, relative to today, there was little that could be done for a seriously ill patient except for support. This meant that ample time remained for bedside manner and for the art of medicine to erupt spontaneously.

Today however, after one hundred years of emerging medical technology, there remains little time or mental space for bedside manner. The mere existence of actionable medical technology renders it "standard of care," so that the weight of scientific consideration becomes a distracting burden.

In lieu of a compelling reason to make room for the clinician's subjective impression, this essential element of decision making becomes a casualty of technology. The doctor-patient interaction no longer occurs by default, as it might have done in Peabody's day, as the computer pulls the clinician away from the bedside.

One still pays lip service to the notion that the agenda of medicine is "caring for the patient." But the scientific rigor of evidence-based medicine has replaced empathy as the central dogma of medical care. The hypnotic illusion of the object as the end-in-itself has replaced the sense that the pre-objective doctor-patient interaction is primary.

Without a model of decision-making that explains how objective knowledge is dependent upon subjective impression, the clinician is left with no theoretical wedge in defense of the doctor-patient interaction. Thereremains no reason to talk to the patient.

A feeble attempt was made in the 20th century to rectify this deficiency by introducing the notion of the "bio-psycho-social" model of medical decision making. This so-called model served to remind the clinician that there are subjective elements of decision-making.

But the "bio-psycho-social" mantra is not a true model. It acknowledges the eclectic sources of the medical decision to make the clinician aware of them, but it does not explain their interaction. It renders no tangible direction to the clinician on how to navigate from subjective impression to objective formulation. It does not materially defend the clinician's beleaguered impulse to make room for the doctor-patient interaction.

The inevitable result is that the bio-psycho-social model has given way to stronger forces. As the complexity and volume of scientific knowledge increases, and as the exigencies of practice management make increasing demands, the clinician is forced to choose objective formulation over the more primal and time-consuming doctor-patient interaction.

The emergence of evidence-based medicine

The model that arose to support this deference to objectivity over subjectivity in decision making is called "evidence-based medicine."

In evidence-based medicine, objective data are construed as the given predicates of a logical proof. The logical necessity of the derived proof is then taken as thenecessary truth of the resulting formulation itself. By this evidence-based model, fidelity to objectivity appears as the sufficient condition of the quality decision.

For this reason, evidence-based medicine brings themedical decision to a premature close. That is, since the decision appears to be "based" on given data as evidence, it appears to require nothing outside of this formulation. It is no longer open to the pre-objective domain of possibility that is accessed as empathy in the doctor-patient interaction.

It is true that rigorous evidence-based formulations render to medicine the benefits of the scientific method: measurability, reproducibility, statistical certainty, and falsifiability (testability). Evidence-based decision making also rescues medicine from the tyranny of historical and institutional authority, by rendering the clinician responsible for demonstrating the elements of the clinical decision.

But the model of evidence-based medicine also

preempts the creative impulse. The clinician may not feel compelled to turn away from the computer screen to engage the patient. The medical decision may come to a premature close in the name of its mere objectivity.

An effective model of decision making therefore must begin with acknowledgement of the background domain of possibility. From this starting point, one then can describe the creative process whereby an evidence- based logical proof emerges in response to subjective perception of possibility. We have called the elements ofthis creative model "possibility theory" and "metaphor induction."

Possibility theory does make room for the role of evidence-based formulation, permitting it to appear to the decision-maker as the end in itself. But it demonstrates, through metaphor induction, that these objective formulations are derived from the subjective impression of possibility in the doctor-patient domain.

Evidence-based formulations thereby can be understood as products of, and therefore as subordinate to, the primary impression of open-ended possibility thatis the milieu of the doctor-patient relationship.

The art and the science of medicine

The mature clinician will develop a sense of her subjective role in the "art" of medicine, even as she can see only the objects of medicine in front of her at anyone time. These two arms of the decision come together in the moment of "discovery" in the medical decision.

For instance, an elderly woman may present to her

doctor with a complaint of swollen, edematous legs. Her doctor might attribute this finding to the failing of her heart in its function as a "pump" in the transfer of blood from her legs to the rest of her body.

This application of the "pump" metaphor does not appear to the clinician as a metaphorical grasp of possibility. Rather, it appears as the grasped possibility itself. It appears to be "discovered" as given. In this moment the art and science of medicine come together.

Understanding the act of discovery simultaneously from these two perspectives, as a creative metaphorical grasp that nevertheless appears as given, uncovers the connection between the art and the science of medicine.

The creation of the object through the application of metaphor is the art of medicine. The appearance of this metaphorical grasp of possibility as the grasped possibility itself is the science of medicine. Thereby the art and the science of medicine merge in the moment experienced as discovery.

By means of this hypnotic aspect of metaphor application, the clinician's devotion to possibility is transferred to the created object itself, as if it were the end-in-itself. This illusion is necessary to precipitate the subject-object interaction whereby intended possibility isactualized. This is the reason that the art of medicine remains occult in the moment of the medical decision.

Good-faith medical decision making

For the clinician who feels bound to "evidence-based medicine" as a sufficient condition of quality medical decision making, there is no escaping the disconnectbetween the art and the science of medicine.

He might feel an artistic impulse in response to patient need, but the evidence-based script with which heworks will awaken in him no acknowledgement of a creative responsibility. All he will see before him is the objective formulation as the end in itself.

This creates the conditions for a moral hazard, that can be expressed in Sartre's terms of "good faith" versus "bad faith," as this pertains to perception of possibility inthe clinical setting.

Devotion to objectivity in "good faith" is devotion to objectivity for that end for which objectivity has come into being: the grasp and actualization of possibility. In this case, the decision-maker will remain responsive to the milieu of the doctor-patient relationship as the sourceand final arbiter of the medical decision.

A devotion to objectivity in "bad faith," on the other hand, is devotion to objectivity as the end in itself, as thesufficient condition of the medical decision. In this case, the user will fail to return to the milieu of the doctor- patient relationship. This is characterized by a premature closure of the medical decision in the name of mere objectivity - and frustration on the part of the patient.

Distinguishing good-faith from bad-faith decision making is difficult because both manifest overtly as devotion to objectivity. However, one is a devotion to objectivity as the means to an end beyond itself, while the other is devotion to objectivity as the end in itself.

Good-faith decision making declares itself in the

existential courage to return to the patient bedside, to respond with creative reformulation of the evidence-based decision.

The medical ethic as a social paradigm

In this way the medical decision requires the clinician to step courageously into the horizon of open-ended possibility, to respond creatively for its actualization. Herein the activity of the clinician is a paradigm of the agenda of medicine as a social institution.

Society cannot hide behind an objective standard in the name of objectivity itself. This is true for any ideology that can be made into a plan of orchestrated behavior. Just as in the case of the physician, the citizen may experience an uneasy ambivalence in response to the realization that every aesthetic, scientific, social, or political system exists ultimately as an existential choice. Social decisions ultimately are "rooted in courage," as Tillich said, for they must render up their claim to being the truth in itself. [73] This realization empowers the clinician, and similarly the citizen, to harness perception of human possibility as the ground of social behavior.

Ultimately, this will require our demonstration of how all objective formulation arises as a creative grasp of open-ended possibility. In the next chapter we will describe this creative process, called metaphor induction, as it applies to the individual medical decision, and anthropologically to medicine in society.

CHAPTER III:
METAPHOR INDUCTION

"Man lives in a symbolic universe."

- Ernst Cassirer, 1944

"From such an organization of the whole of experience derived the acceptance of what seem to us somewhat strange analogies. It was possible to argue from one part of the cosmic hierarchy to another; to define the relations of father to family or of pope to emperor, from the superiority of the heart to the limbs or the sun to the moon. And once a correspondence had been established it had all the compulsion of eternal and inescapable truth." [205]

-Denys Hay, The Medieval Centuries, 1964

The basic structure of metaphor induction

Metaphor induction is our name for the creative process at the foundation of medical decision making. The process of metaphor induction brings together two features of the medical decision: the application of metaphor to grasp possibility as an object for the subject in mind; and the hypnotic impression of this object as the grasped possibility itself, such that the subject's devotion to possibility is transferred to the object itself as the end in itself. This sets up the conditions for the subject-object interaction whereby possibility, in which both subject and object partake, is actualized.

There are many ways one might analyze this creative process. One might simply list all its features as if they were the sequential steps whereby objective data and their coherent structure emerge in mind from the application of metaphor. However, this does not address the various ways in which metaphor accommodates the anthropic contingencies of knowing.

Therefore, rather than simply listing these features as sequential steps, we will consider each feature as it addresses some contingency of knowing. We will call these individual features "metaphor functions."

Each metaphor function is characterized either by a specific kind of metaphor, or a manner in which the metaphor is used to satisfy a specific contingency of knowing. These functions are not mutually exclusive; They complement each other and occur in combination.

Kinds of metaphor function

Let us begin by naming and briefly describing eight metaphor functions that are basic to metaphor induction. No doubt a thorough phenomenological investigation would render more than these eight functions.

1. The <u>gestalt function</u>: This is the ad-hoc application of a root metaphor (a term borrowed from Stephen Pepper) to a region of intended possibility in its entirety, so that its basic elements, including its intended ends and the means to them, are described in terms of the categories of this metaphor. Examples of

such root metaphors are the "electromagnetic field" in physics, or "historical materialism" in political theory, or "humoral balance" or the "genome" in medicine.

2. The <u>coherence function:</u> This is the integration of all the features of a realm of possibility that results when they are described in terms of the categories of a single metaphor. Thereby, the features appear to lead back to this one applied root metaphor, from which they were derived, as their necessary conclusion. The formulation is then susceptible to taking the form of a logical argument or a formal or informal proof.

3. The <u>induction function:</u> This is the hypnotic phenomenon wherein the object that is created by the application of a metaphor appears discovered as given. The metaphorical grasp of possibility thereby appears as the grasped possibility itself. The subject's devotion to possibility thereby is transferred to the created object as if it were the intended end in itself. This creates the conditions for the subject-object interaction whereby intended possibility, as the common ground of subject and object, is actualized.

4. The <u>intentional function:</u> This is the choice of a metaphor to model a specific trajectory of intention regarding an area of intended possibility. An example is Plato's "angler" metaphor to describe the sophist as an opportunist, or the physicist's "wave" metaphor

to accommodate quantum probability.

5. The <u>anthropic function:</u> This is the choice of a metaphor that accommodates the contingencies of knowing, so that the product emerges as a well-formed object for the subject. Examples of this kind of metaphor are the "atom" of physics or the "molecule" of genetics, as each accommodates analysis in terms of identical units, or the open-ended "phenotype" of molecular biology to accommodate the perspectival grasp of possibility in terms of distinct "traits."

6. The <u>framing function:</u> This is the repeated application of a single metaphorical formulation to multiple and diverse areas of possibility. These re- provisioned metaphorical formulations are called the "laws" of nature, as they are posited to exist in the domain of reality, wherein they are said to be found. Objective formulations of diverse areas are constructed in terms of their discovery as instances of these laws. In this way, all of possibility can be integrated in terms of a finite set of metaphors. An example of this is the law of the "conservation of energy" as it applies to all closed physical systems.

7. The <u>formative function:</u> This is the application of metaphor to accommodate the formative influence of perception of possibility upon the knowing subject. In that the subject is ontologically the perceiver of possibility, the encounter and reaction to possibility has a

formative effect. Awareness of this condition of existence is experienced as the "moral" sense. To accommodate this effect, metaphor is modified with terms, such as "should" or "ought," that combine the future tense with a sense of obligation, and thereby a reference to responsibility to possibility.

8. The <u>reconciliation function</u>: The subject is a manifestation of the cosmic domain of possibility that she shares with the object. But she has been estranged from this common ground by its bifurcation in mind into a knowing subject and known world. Therefore, she requires reconciliation with this ground, to understand her identity and role as subject with regard to this cosmic domain. This reconciliation is accommodated by metaphors that grasp the domain of possibility in its entirety, and in a form with which the subject can interact. For this, metaphors arise such as the Hindu "Brahman" or the Buddhist "Dharma" or the Chinese "Tao" or the unitary "God" of the monotheistic religions, or the impersonal ordered universe of Spinoza.

Let us now look at each of these metaphor functions in detail.

The *gestalt* metaphor function

The power of a root metaphor to grasp an entire range of intended possibility lies partly in the richness of its potential sub-categories. When a range of possibility, such as a branch of physics or a field of clinical research, submits to the parameters of an applied root metaphor, its intended beginning, and its end, and the causal links between them, are formulated in terms of the categories of this root metaphor.

Stephen Pepper famously described this process in his "root metaphor" theory of cosmology, in which he said that the theorist "pitches upon some area of commonsense fact and tries if he cannot understand other areas in terms of this one." [78] The structural characteristics of the applied metaphor become the basic concepts of description and explanation for everything grasped as an object in the intended range of possibility.

The choice of a root metaphor arises from the subject's intuition that the range of possibility, including its intended end, and the causal steps to it, can be unified in terms of the categories of the applied metaphor. As Eddington said of this process in physics, "our problem becomes inverted - we have not to discover theproperties of a thing which we have recognized in nature, but to discover how to recognize in nature a thingwhose properties we have assigned." [10]

Not all of possibility will come to us naturally and easily within the terms of the selected root metaphor. Rather, we approach possibility in terms of the metaphor for the sake of its organizing potential. As Eddington said, we "select a form which we ourselves have prescribed, and treat the rest as contamination which we can remove." [79] Or, as the mathematician

George Polya famously said of geometry, it is "the science of correct reasoning on incorrect figures." [50]

The hazard of reductionism

Root metaphors of a cosmological nature, such as molecular biology, are taken to be a description of the basic elements of reality itself. Therefore, one assumes that they can provide an exhaustive account of any phenomenon that is described in their terms. For instance, when a medical illness is described in terms of molecular biology, one assumes that the formulation has captured all that can be said of that illness, as it is described in terms of the basic features of reality itself.

This assumption creates the intellectual hazard of reductionism. William James illustrated the hazard of reduction in his famous example of a Beethoven quartet. He pointed out that a quartet can be exhaustively described as "a scraping of horses' tails on cats' bowels." [51]

Beethoven. *Susan Saandholland on Midjourney*

If one takes this physical-reductive metaphor as the elements of what is real in the world, it will then appear to have grasped the essential and entire truth of the performance of the quartet. The experience of the Beethoven quartet will appear, in theory, to be reducible to this physical metaphor.

But this description of a Beethoven quartet seems insufficient to us. We recognize features of the musical encounter that elude the boundaries of the cat-gut-on-horse-hair metaphor. One simply cannot do justice to thephenomenon of music as it is experienced in terms of thephysical interactions of cat and horse tissue. Our perception of musical possibility, as it is apprehended, does not admit of this.

This illustrates that just because a phenomenon

can be reduced to a metaphor does not mean that the boundaries of that metaphor are adequate to the full range of possibility perceived therein.

This is the case with all metaphors as metaphor. This is not because they are insufficient metaphors but because, as metaphor, they are perspectival and not sufficient to the infinite domain of possibility.

In one sense a Beethoven quartet is entirely reducible to the black dots on tablature paper. The notes appear given to the musician as the musical ends in themselves. But the experience that is produced by the performer, as she interacts with these dots, is an end richer in possibility. That is, the dots, by appearing to the subject as the ends in themselves, precipitate a subject-object interaction whereby a more deeply-apprehended possibility is actualized.

The black dots of tablature are the utilitarian terms of causality whereby the true causality of the actualization of possibility is executed. The thoughtful musician knows implicitly that the composer intended something more expansive. She senses the dots as a means of actualizing this end. She does not mistake the dots on thepage with the music itself.

Similarly, the script of molecular biology acts as a "musical score" for the clinician. It gives him access to possibility manifested in the patient. Its molecules are the black dots with which he will interact, to actualize the human possibility that is apprehended directly in the doctor-patient interaction.

The scientist practicing molecular biology is like the musician performing Beethoven. The molecules of gene theory serve to grasp the subjective experience of biologic life in the same way that the black notes printed on tablature serve to grasp the subjective experience of the musician. They are an objective means to an end beyond themselves, through their interaction with the subject.

The limits of metaphor

An example of this is the class of monoclonal antibody called the SGLT-inhibitors, that emerged in theearly 21st century to treat diabetes mellitus.

Creation of this drug began with the observation that there is a natural "receptor" in the kidney that helps to maintain a normal glucose level in the blood. It does this by capturing glucose as it passes from the blood into the kidneys, then returning this glucose to the bloodstream before it can be cleared from the kidneys into the urine. This protein, called the SGLT receptor, thereby helps to recycle glucose back to the patient's blood, so as to help maintain a normal blood glucose level.

The problem in a patient with diabetes mellitus is that the blood glucose already is too high. To take advantage of the function of the SGLT receptor, a molecule was engineered to block the glucose-capturing activity of the SGLT receptor in the kidney. This permits glucose to pass on through the kidney, to be cleared in the urine. This has the effect of lowering the glucose in the blood of a diabetic patient.

This new drug does in fact treat high glucose in the diabetic patient, and it renders the expected clinical benefits related to this. As defined within the boundaries of its formulated molecular theory, this would appear to be the beginning and the end of it.

However, this drug proved to have several side effects that were not anticipated by the molecular model of the drug as it first was conceived. Some of these side effects are unwanted. These include genital infections, elevated cholesterol, metabolic acidosis, and bone fractures. None of these would appear to have anything to do with blood glucose or its clearing.

The use of molecular formulations therefore requires a realization that these formulations, though they appear exhaustive, are in fact perspectival. They sometimes miss as much possibility as they grasp. The clinician must remain sensitive to the background of human possibility apprehended directly in the doctor-patient relationship, rather than relying solely on the molecular model as formulated. The clinician must be a good "musician," as it were, alert to the inherent limitations of the molecular model as metaphor.

In medicine, as in physics, we fabricate objectivity at the cost of distorting what is seen. We partition possibility within the boundaries of limited perspective, represented by the chosen metaphor.

Eddington discussed this perspectival distortion in his example of the prism refraction of light into its component wave lengths. In one sense this regularity is introduced into the study of light, since the spectroscope interferes with light. That is, it is unclear "whether the spectroscope finds or whether it makes the green color which it shows us." [90]

The anthropic origin of a gestalt metaphor

The choice of a metaphor to serve a gestalt function is based on a sense that it will apply to all aspects of the intended range of possibility. This universal application cannot be known empirically ahead of time. The only way this can be anticipated is through a tacit awareness of the anthropic conditions of knowing as they will apply to the intended range of possibility. In its application to all knowing, it will apply to all that is known. In this way the choice of gestalt metaphor says more about the conditions of knowing than about the known. As Eddington stated, the mind demands "by its 'necessities of thought' certain qualities in the parts which make up the physical universe." [93]

An example of this is the emergence of the "quantum" as a root metaphor for the new physics of the 20th century. The century opened with the assumption that all of physical reality can be known in terms of massand energy. These two terms are posited as fundamental because they accommodate the anthropic need in every instance to grasp possibility as material interaction.

These two terms, of mass and energy, can be measured fundamentally in terms of radiation. Further, Max Planck found empirically that radiation manifests inevery instance of its measurement by a limiting unit that he called the "quantum." Thus, the quantum was a wayof measuring radiation, and so of mass and energy, and so of all physical reality. Thereby, the quantum revealed itself as a candidate root metaphor for all of physical reality.

Eddington described Planck's innovation as an "instinct" that the quantum is "something lying at the root of the world-structure... a starting-point for a radical revision of the classical conception." [79]

But Planck did not know ahead of time that all of reality could be reduced to the quantum. This would be impossible empirically. What he knew ahead of time was that all of reality could be defined in terms of the limiting measurement of the quantum, for it was a condition of reference to radiation, that was itself a way to define mass and energy. Therefore, it can be said that Planck's "instinct" was as much about the anthropic contingencies of knowing as it was about known reality.

In a more mundane example, by the 20th century the vehicle for the exchange of value, called "money," appeared to apply to any measure of economic activity. Therefore, money came to serve as a root metaphor of economic activity, creating the paradigm "monetarism." When it became apparent later in the 20th century that value exchange can occur independent of money, this root metaphor fell away as no longer serving a gestalt function.

The root metaphor in a paradigm shift

As Capra pointed out, modern science rediscovered what was observed by the Eastern mystic, that all concepts that describe nature are inherently limited in relation to the infinity of the whole. Therefore, these concepts "are not features of reality, as we tend to believe, but creations of the mind; parts of the map, not of the territory." [81] In time, every metaphor, such as "money" or the "atom" or the "molecule" or a particular "diagnosis," manifests the limits of its finite boundaries when applied to the infinite domain of possibility.

As Stephen Toulmin described, the language of science at any one time takes the form of a hierarchy of terms that continually shift at a level superficial to the root metaphors upon which they are based. On occasion however the "superstructure has to be knocked down too" and settled terms are swept away. [82] This process was famously described by Thomas Kuhn in his notionof the "paradigm shift."

When a root metaphor reaches its point of natural limitation in the grasp of possibility, modification of the formulation must then take place at this fundamental level. The mind recedes into a permissive mode, in a posture that Husserl called the "bracketing" of a current viewpoint, and a new root metaphor emerges for gestalt application, replacing the former root metaphor.

For instance, Eddington documented the shift from Newtonian physics to relativity theory in the 20th century in terms of a displacement of their core notions. He noted that the deflection of light when passing a massive body was not well explained by the notion of a "force" tugging on a wave, as in the old paradigm. Nowa different metaphor was needed to explain this observation. So, the notion of the "curvature of space" replaced the Newtonian notion of "force." Eddington described this shift as the supplanting of metaphors...

Newtonian law told us of the amount of the tug and there is now no tug to be considered. Since the phenomenon is now pictured as curvature the new law must say something about curvature... But our main reason for rejecting Newton's law is not its imperfect accuracy... it is because it does not contain the kind of information about Nature thatwe want to know... Einstein's law of gravitation controls a geometrical quantity 'curvature' in contrast to Newton's law which controls a mechanical quantity 'force.' [83]

The paradigm shift in medicine

Similarly, a paradigm shift is taking place in our own time in medicine. We are moving away from a conception of illness as discrete entities of disease that exist in the body where they are to be found, and to a notion, instead, of molecular mutation manifesting as aberrant "phenotypes."

Just as the notion of the "balance of humors" was abandoned as an explanation of health and illness, we gradually will discard the reified notion of illness as discrete "entities of disease" existing in the body to be found. We will in time replace this notion with the new paradigm of molecular biology.

Phenotype. *Susan Saandholland on Midjourney*

The root metaphor of molecular biology, in its more simple form, is what Francis Crick called the "central dogma" of the gene. The "gene," as the unit of heredity, was defined by Crick as a dedicated strand of DNA that codes for a specific protein product. Life is said to be a manifestation of the interaction of distinct protein molecules, each derived from a dedicated DNA strand in the nucleus of every cell. All features of life, conceived of as various "traits," such as gender, eye color, body habitus, personality and even consciousness, are taken to be the result, directly or indirectly, of these protein products, specifically of their interactions as determined by their three-dimensional structure and electrical charge.

Therefore, by knowing the protein products

involved in a life process, and identifying their genetic loci and their DNA sequence, a researcher is presumed to possess the tools she needs to understand and to influence any feature of life.

For instance, using the new molecular engineering technique known as CRISPR ("clustered regularly-interspaced short palindromic repeats"), a researcher can directly edit a targeted strand of DNA within a living organism, thereby altering its protein product, and the related phenotypic manifestation.

At the time of this writing, CRISPR has been used in laboratory rats to modify the gene responsible for Duchenne muscular dystrophy. This gene produces a protein component of the cytoskeletal structure of muscle cells called "dystrophin." Thus, the DNA sequence found to code for this protein also is called the "dystrophin" gene. When the dystrophin protein shape is abnormal, due to a mutation in the dystrophin gene, there results a weakness and atrophy of the muscles. CRISPR has been used in live rats to repair the dystrophin gene, resulting in a healthy dystrophin protein, thus curing the laboratory rat of muscular dystrophy.

As such techniques give us improved access to human health, we no longer will need to think of illness in terms of distinct entities of disease that exist in the body to be found. Instead, "health" will be conceived of as the interaction of proteins from genes that have evolved over time to their current wild state. "Illness" will be conceived of as a mutation of this evolved state, resulting in aberrant protein products and their perturbedinteractions.

In the new paradigm of molecular biology, the notion of a discoverable "disease entity" will be supplanted by the notion of a manifesting "phenotype." A phenotype is the trait that results either from the wild type (evolved)or the mutated protein product. The phenotype is said to result causally from the genotype.

One begins analysis by assuming in each instance the existence of a genotype as the cause of a subjectively-defined phenotype. One then works backwards, in an ad hoc manner, to build the molecular formulation in terms of finding the hypostatized genetic locus.

Already we find that, just as the notion of the particle in quantum theory has manifested its limitations, so in molecular biology the notion of the "gene" manifests its limitations, requiring the notion of an "epi-genome."

For instance, despite the central dogma of the gene, defined by Francis Crick as a dedicated strand of DNA producing a single protein product, one now observes that a strand of DNA is not limited to spawning a single protein product. A cell can select different combinations of the same DNA strand to make different proteins, a phenomenon called "alternative splicing." It is estimated that the average DNA strand produces over five different transcripts, and thus different proteins, through this process of alternate splicing.

What is "directing" this selection process if it is not the single strand of DNA itself? This observation would seem to belie the notion of the gene as it is defined by the central dogma.

To salvage the notion of the gene as the unit of

heredity, it appears necessary either to redefine the gene as something other-than a dedicated DNA-to-protein unit, or one must posit an "epi-genetic" process that directs the gene from outside the gene unit.

The limits of the molecular metaphor have led us to question the reduction of life to an interaction of proteins coded for by DNA. Are our molecular formulations capable of an exhaustive account of life? Do they define the limits of life, or do they reflect the anthropic limits of our understanding of life at this time? Should they be understood as perspectival tools circumscribed by the boundaries of the "molecular" narrative? Should we appreciate that there might be more fundamental ways of understanding physiologic processes and that will come to us in time, such as quantum-level communication at a cellular level, the effects of which we see at this time only as they manifest as molecular interactions?

One should not approach medical diagnosis and treatment based simply on the terms of molecular biology any more than one would turn over the performance of a Beethoven quartet to a novice musician, who only can read music tablature but not interpret it. Molecular biology is not the "music itself" of life. It is the tablature, the anthropic means to the music of life. It is a map, not the landscape.

We should ask whether the molecular model is our window to a larger process that has evolved to more fundamentally anticipate possibility itself at a higher level, and so to respond in real time to changing conditions as they manifest.

All theory, in that it is based on metaphor, must be understood as grasping possibility in this perspectival way, defined explicitly by the boundaries of the metaphor. The metaphor itself does not alert the user to its own limitations, to the fact that there is a larger domain of possibility outside its boundaries. One must appreciate this limitation implicitly when applying the gestalt role of metaphor.

The necessity of metaphor

The metaphorical structure of medical science does not mean that its objects are "not real," for instance that the heart is "not really a pump" or that drugs are "not really coded information." This objection would serve only to treat metaphor in a counter-productive way.

Furthermore, this would imply that there is a privileged, non-metaphorical, perspective. There is no such privileged perspective, nor is there any reason to wish for one. The metaphorically-contrived formulation emerges to serve an end beyond itself in the grasp and actualization of possibility, apprehended directly in the doctor-patient relationship.

The *coherence* metaphor function

The chosen root metaphor donates its constituent categories to the emerging objective formulation. In this way it renders an overall coherence and interdependence of terminology to the formulation. This creative process is shepherded into being by the intention to actualize perceived possibility, and it is the core mechanism of what broadly has come to be called "calculation."

This begins with the gestalt function, wherein a root metaphor, such as an "angler," or the "atom" or the "wave" or the "field" in physics, or the "gene" or a specific "diagnosis" in medicine, is applied to grasp a circumscribed realm of possibility. Then the mind works backwards, to creatively grasp finer detail of possibility in terms of the categories of the applied root metaphor.

The resulting coherent formulation renders causal links for the utilitarian grasp and actualization of the intended range of possibility.

The metaphorically-formulated data of the system are experienced as "discovered," and are therefore construed as "findings." In this form they appear to lead back to the root metaphor, from which they were derived, as their necessary conclusion. This leads to conceiving of these findings as "evidence," so that the structure of the medical decision assumes the form of an "evidence-based" proof.

For instance, a patient might present to her doctor with a red rash on her arms and legs. The physician knows that this rash might be explained by any number of diagnoses. It might be due to a systemic vasculitis affecting the blood vessels, or to a vascular flair of hormonal over-activity as in pheochromocytoma, or the petechial leakage of blood associated with platelet insufficiency, or to a viral infection, or to an infection such as Rocky Mountain Spotted Fever or Lyme disease, or the embolic phenomena of endocarditis, etc.

This set of different organizing diagnoses, all candidates for root metaphors of the system, is called in medicine the "differential diagnosis." By testing how the categories associated each diagnosis accommodate the possibility inherent in the situation, the doctor makes a progressive selection of the more effective "fit" - as the finer details of a symptom complex are integrated as a theoretical whole in terms of current physiologic theory.

For instance, upon finding autoimmune antibodies in the blood of the patient above, the doctor might feel that this rash could represent an "autoimmune vasculitis"associated with systemic lupus erythematosus (SLE). As this metaphorical grasp of possibility appears discoveredas the clinical possibility itself, the decision will be fashioned as an "evidence-based" argument, and the rash "proven to be" an autoimmune vasculitis. The logical necessity of the formulation is therein taken to establish the necessary truth of the clinical assessment.

From the perspective of possibility theory, the truth in this coherent formulation lies in its utility in the grasp and actualization of clinical possibility.

The *induction* metaphor function

As we have seen, the application of metaphor to grasp possibility as an object for the subject has a "hypnotic" effect.

The new object appears not as a metaphorical grasp of possibility, but as the grasped possibility itself. It appears discovered as "given." This represents a transfer of the subject's devotion, from the perceived possibility, to the created object with which it is grasped, now appearing as the intended end in itself. To underscore the hypnotic aspect of this effect, we use the term metaphor "induction."

This hypnotic process is necessary to precipitate the resulting subject-object interaction whereby possibility is actualized. This manifests as the scientific process.

Metaphor induction as Socratic method

This hypnotic aspect of metaphor manifests in the Socratic method of teaching. We can review how this is employed in Plato's dialogue, The Meno.

In The Meno, Socrates presumes to teach geometry to a slave boy. He does this by drawing a figure in the sand and directing the slave boy's attention to it as a geometrical figure. Socrates asks several onlookers to take note that the slave boy will appear to recover from "within himself" the principles of geometry, "though I simply ask him questions without teaching him." [85] In so doing, Socrates surreptitiously introduces the metaphor of the square to the slave boy.

Socrates asks the slave boy a series of questions regarding the four-sided image he has drawn in the sand, using terms derived from the constituent parts of the geometric image of a "square." Even as we describe this event, the figure drawn in the sand by Socrates appears in our imagination as "given" as a square, once he has referred to it as such.

Slave Boy and Square. *Susan Saandholland on Midjourney*

It is important to note that Socrates might have referred to this image with any number of metaphors that are not geometric, per se, and regarding which Socrates might have wished to teach the slave boy, such as a time frame, or a terrain map, or a weather pattern, or the connected axioms of a logical argument, or simply the characteristics of moving soft sand about with a stick.

In this case, the questions posed to the boy serve to enjoin his involvement with the possibilities inherent in the image as a geometrical figure, that is, in terms of the constituent parts of a square. Specifically, the slave boy is asked whether the "area" of this square might be determined by knowing its "diagonal."

To the amazement of all onlookers, the slave boy eventually provides the correct answer. He is led to the answer by the inherent coherence of the categories of thesquare, introduced to him on the sly by questions posed to him by Socrates.

As the categories of the applied square appear to the boy, and to the onlookers, as given at the moment of their application, it appears that the slave boy somehow knew the answers ahead of time. Socrates says, "these opinions were somewhere in him, were they not?"

To account for a slave boy appearing spontaneously to know the intricacies of geometry, Socrates invokes the notion of a prior life of an immortal soul. Socrates posits that "the truth about reality is always in our soul," so that knowledge is essentially "recollecting or remembering."

Of course, what was "in" the slave boy is the perception of possibility that he shares with others. The specific metaphor with which possibility is grasped is not "given." It is a creative choice, rendered to the slave boy by Socrates in the form of the questions posed to him. This is the same Socratic method of teaching usedin modern medical education.

Metaphor induction in scientific terminology

Eddington discussed this utilitarian use of geometryin the natural sciences as an illustration of the volitional origin of the terms of objective science.

In his book on the mathematical foundation of relativity theory Eddington discussed the advantage of applying geometric figures to the problems of physical science, pointing out that thereby... "an extensive geometrical nomenclature becomes available... straight line, gradient, curvature, etc... and a self-explanatory nomenclature is a considerable aid in discussing an abstruse subject... electric force, potential, temperature, etc.; we may draw the isotherms as straight lines, ellipses, spheres, according to convenience." [200]

Once a geometrical model has been applied to a domain of study, it appears not as a metaphorical grasp of this field, but as the grasped possibility itself. As Eddington said...

"... we habitually think of them graphically, and are almost unconscious that there is anything conventional in the way we represent them. For example, measured distances and directions are instinctively conceived by us graphically [even though] these quantities are not in their intrinsic nature dissimilar from other physical quantities which are not habitually represented geometrically... If we eliminated the human element... the device of graphical representation of the results of measures or estimates of distances would appear just as artificial as the graphical representation of thermometer readings." [200]

Often it is easier to recognize the volitional origin of metaphor in the sciences from a historical perspective, as we have moved on by then to other metaphors that have taken over the mantel of the given.

For example, the historian Elizabeth Patterson, in her account of the origin of the atomic theory of chemistry in the 18th century, described the initial reservations with the atomic hypothesis as "a reluctance to accept as the 'elements of chemical combination' any metaphysical entities such as were atoms.'" [132] However, once the actions of gases were explained by John Dalton in terms of their "atomic weight," the atomic nature of chemistry was made to appear discovered as given, and the atomic notion no longer to appear as metaphor.

Similarly, as related by the historian of mathematics Morris Kline, the reduction of the harmony of vibrating strings to numerical relations by the Greeks lent itself to analysis of the orbital periods of the planets forming a kind of musical scale, making a "harmony of the spheres." [88] The notion of harmony thereby served to organize the phenomena of planetary motion.

This reduction did not appear to the ancient Greeks as a metaphorical grasp of the possibilities inherent in planetary movement, but as the planetary motion itself, that is, as another instance of "harmony."

Even in physics today the notion of harmony remains a valuable metaphor. As Capra pointed out, the reason that the short-lived hadron particles are called "resonances is related to an analogy that can be drawn to the well-known resonance phenomenon encountered in connection with vibrations." [89]

The recognition of this reifying feature of metaphor is ancient. It is captured in the Hindu concept called "maya" in Sanskrit. Maya is the illusion that our terms for things around us and their objective characteristics are the reality of nature, "instead of realizing that they are concepts of our measuring and categorizing minds," as Capra put it. [86]

The artifacts of reified metaphors document the history of medicine in a way that reveals the hypnotic feature of metaphor induction.

An example is the isolation in 1975 of a human protein that was called the "tumor necrosis factor" because it was found to help the immune system to kill cancer cells. The gene that was found to code for this protein also received the name the "tumor necrosis factor" gene.

This ad hoc naming of a genetic locus prior to its discovery helps to guide formulation of the genotype, in terms of its "discovery," toward a tool for actualizing the possibility grasped by the phenotype. However, it also reifies the subjective impression, so that future modifications of the name of the genetic locus and of its protein products are constrained.

For instance, the "tumor necrosis factor" protein is known now to have a much wider role in several pathologic processes in the body, such as autoimmune colitis and psoriatic arthritis, that do not pertain to cancer. Thus, monoclonal antibodies to this tumor necrosis factor have been manufactured to treat these other illnesses. But we still refer to this protein as the "tumor necrosis factor," as these are the terms in which itfirst was conceived.

As time goes by, the names of objects in the genome come to reflect their historical lineage as much as their function. This evolving disconnect between name and function merely underscores the intrenched perspectival origin of the metaphors of molecular biology.

The *intentional* metaphor function

The selection of a metaphor to model a specific trajectory of intention regarding a range of possibility, such as Plato's grasp of the sophist as an "angler," we will call the "intentional" metaphor function.

In this case the applied metaphor provides the cognitive scaffolding whereby the mind can grasp intended possibility. It will define what counts as data, and it will create terms of measurement and the logical predicates of coherence whereby causality is invoked.

An example in quantum theory is how the metaphor of the "wave" is engaged to accommodate probabilities pertaining to mass and energy. This metaphor, in the mathematical form of the "wave function," permits measurement and prediction. As Eddington said, regarding the notion of the wave, "we are as it were making our adopted basis of a priori probability a constituent of the world-structure - adding to the world akind of symbolic texture." [87]

The language of medical science similarly can be understood as a fabric of interwoven metaphors. These arise in each case from an existential decision regarding what aspect of possibility is intended for actualization, and the trajectory of intention regarding it.

So, the notion of the heart as a "pump" brings the categories of cyclic fluid dynamics to bear upon cardiac illness, and the notion of drugs as "chemically coded information" brings to bear the categories of code storage and transport. The deployment of the notions of "signaling," and "anti-bodies," and "response to threat" are brought to bear in immunologic disease as conditionsof molecular interaction, just as the notion of the "propagation of action potential" along charged channelsis brought to bear in neurology.

The application of metaphor often is experienced by the clinician as the sensation that she "recognizes" the diagnosis in a patient. This is the feeling of the grasp of the intended possibility inherent in a clinical situation.

The structure of possibility gradually reveals itself in its resistance to the applied metaphor, within the subject-object interaction. This resistance will result in a dialectical revision of the intended object, contrived as ongoing "discovery" of the diagnosis.

The *anthropic* metaphor function

In the same way that the "intentional" metaphor function accommodates a specific trajectory of intention, so likewise a metaphor can be chosen to accommodate the anthropic contingencies of grasping possibility as an object for the subject. We will call this the "anthropic" metaphor function.

It is no surprise that the objective components of natural science contain subjective elements. It could not be otherwise. The object exists for the subject. Thus, it must be formed as an object with respect to the subject.

The characteristics that we posit as existing in the external world, where they are to be found, are chosen from our intuited awareness of our own cognitive needs and limitations in objective knowing. Let us consider a simple illustration.

The lyre as example of the anthropic function

In fourth-century BC the stringed musical instrument called the lyre was a source of terms with which music was performed. The note of the musical scale that was played on the first string of the lyre was called "lichanos." This word in the Greek means "forefinger," as this is the finger with which this string was plucked on the lyre.

To the fourth-century musician the note named "lichanos" was not a metaphorical grasp of the tone or its manner of performance. It was just the note itself. It is the note that we today call "G" on the musical scale, defined by us in terms of the alphabet. Just as this note is "G" for us today, it was "lichanos" for the musician then. In this way its anthropic feature served to create a well-formed object for the subject. Its very name helped to precipitate the subject-object interaction, of forefinger on string, whereby musical possibility was actualized.

Lyre. *Susan Saandholland on Midjourney*

Any metaphor might have been chosen for this note on the lyre. The "lichanos" metaphor was chosen for its anthropic function, just as naming notes after letters of the alphabet does for us today. It was chosen not because it accommodated a specific trajectory of intention - not to play a specific tune - but because it accommodated any and all music-making possibilities on the lyre.

The anthropic function in science

Similarly, Eddington pointed out that atomic theory arises from our anthropic need to analyze experience in terms of identical, recurring units. [36] He underscored the anthropic origin of atomic theory, saying that it is an "ingrained" form of thought, so that the aim of physical analysis is to "resolve the universe into structural units which are precisely like one another." [92]

The "atom," from the Greek *atomos* (non-divisible), is by this definition the smallest component of physical reality. It brings together the notions of "size" and "divisibility" into one metaphor. These notions require a knowing subject for their meaning, but they are posited as characteristics of the objects themselves. As an anthropic feature of knowing it could be made to applyto all instances of knowing and thus made into an organizing feature of all of reality.

There is nothing, in itself, about searching for the smallest, indivisible elements of reality that is necessary for analyzing reality. It is a useful anthropic manner of grasping reality. It is true that by defining common features of the smallest building blocks, we fashion a way of describing common features of all of reality. But it might be that higher-level features of reality that emerge or manifest from these smallest elements are in fact the fundamental, if latent, elements in the end. In looking for the smallest physical elements, our manner of research might miss these fundamental elements.

This atomic hypothesis was posited by Democritus centuries before anything could be said to be "discovered" as an atom. Therefore, the ancient belief that reality has an atomic structure was based not upon what was known about reality, but upon the intuited contingencies of knowing. As Eddington said, the laws of nature, in that they arise to accommodate the structure of thought, "can be discovered a priori by scrutinizing the frame of thought." [38]

Eddington enumerated several examples of the reifying of anthropic contingencies of knowing into the structure of reality in this ad hoc manner. Regarding the notion of a physical world itself, for instance, he said that if we take "observation" as a requirement of the given, we "impose a selective test on the knowledge which is admitted." [95] That is, we posit a material world as the discoverable world because "material" is our term for the subject's ability to grasp and manipulate.

Democritus Atomic Hypothesis. *Susan Saandholland on Midjourney*

Similarly, the notion of "substance" accommodates our need for permanence of objects. As Eddington said...

The element of permanence in the physical world, which is familiarly represented by the conception of substance, is essentially a contribution of the mind to the plan of building or selection... In this sense the value placed on permanence creates the world of apparent substance. [96]

In addition to a "physical" and "substantive" world, Eddington suggested the notion of the self-sufficiency ofatomic elements as "an epistemological consequence of the frame of thought which requires the elementary physical systems to be isolable and yet observable."

He also mentioned the co-existence of elementary parts, and the "law of conservation" (of mass, energy, momentum, electric charge) as anthropic contributions to the foundation of physics. [97]

These anthropic metaphors arise not because we have discovered them ahead of time to be features of the discoverable world in every instance, but because they accommodate the contingencies of knowing as they are intuited ahead of time, and are therefore projected into the frame of the world so that it can be known by us.

The application of anthropic metaphor

The creation of an objective formulation by the application of the categories of the atomic metaphor, such as size and divisibility, is construed as "finding" these atomic features in reality. By first positing an atomic structure into reality, the objects discovered therein take on these anthropic features.

It may seem that the introduction of these anthropic features into objects of science is an impurity; for truth classically is taken to be devoid of subjective influence. But the knowing subject is no less a part of the elementalstuff of the universe than is the known object. Therefore, the anthropic contingencies of knowing that make their way into the structure of the object also represent the structure of reality, no less than does the known object.

As Eddington said...

We cannot say that the rainbow, as part of the world, was meant to convey the vivid effects of color; butwe can perhaps say that the human mind as part ofthe world was meant to perceive it that way. [156]

It was the genius of relativity theory to unite the subject and the object into their common ground by redefining the objects of science in such a way as to make reference to their subjective conditions. As Heisenberg famously said, what we observe is "nature exposed to our method of questioning." [39] Similarly, as an example, Eddington pointed out that probability, as it is represented in wave mechanics in physics, is "frankly subjective, being relative to the knowledge which we happen to possess." [40]

Thus, we start our scientific analysis not by asking whether the structure of reality is atomic, but by asking "what is the atomic structure" of reality? This forces our formulation of theory, in terms of its "discovery," into an atomic frame. As Eddington said, "in the discovery of this system of law the mind may be regarded as regaining from Nature that which the mind has put into nature." [94]

For instance, when we propose to investigate the "molecular" foundation of oncology, or endocrinology, or neurology, or immunology, we are rendering an ad hoc anthropic molecular framework to them, whereby the possibility that they represent can be grasped and actualized.

The evolution of anthropic root metaphors

As atomic theory grows over time, its metaphorical terms evolve to better accommodate the possibility that it seeks to grasp.

This does not mean that the created object, such as

the atom or the gene, increasingly assumes or mirrors thestructure of possibility in its own form. Rather, the object evolves to become a better object-for the subject, that is, for interaction with the subject to accommodate the goal of actualizing possibility through the resulting subject-object interaction. We will explore the evolution of the notion of the atom, as well as of the gene, and its notion of DNA in more detail in the next chapter.

The *framing* metaphor function

The "laws" of nature emerge in natural science fromthe capacity of the mind to extrapolate from one instanceof gestalt metaphor induction to multiple other areas. In this way, exploration of the infinite domain of possibility can be unified under the rubric of a finite number of root metaphors.

Thereby we make reality in our image, so that it can be known by us. Or, more precisely, the universe comes to know itself through the agency of the evolved brain, through this framing function.

To the subject, this act of universal framing appears as the "finding" of a common set of laws throughout all of nature. In actuality, the mind formulates nature in terms of these laws. This extrapolation is possible if the trajectory of intention that was grasped with the index metaphor can be made to apply to other areas of possibility.

For example, "harmony" was first described as the mathematical relations of strings of relative lengths. This pattern of intention offered itself also as a way to imagine, before the notion of gravity, the relative orbital periods of the known planets.

We noted also that there are different kinds of laws.

There are those that apply to specific trajectories of intention, such as the Pythagorean theorem, and those that apply to all instances of knowledge because they capture the contingencies of knowing itself.

These latter are called the "laws of nature," for they apply anywhere reality is to be described by an observer. As Eddington said regarding these laws of nature, the scientific observers "become aware beforehand of limitations to which the results they obtain will have to conform... and, unaware of their subjective origin, hail them as laws of nature." [149]

By accepting such laws as given, we are agreeing implicitly to structure our world within their boundaries. Not all of possibility will come to us easily within the metaphorical terms of these laws. We approach possibility within the latitude that they provide.

Examples of metaphorical framing as law

To analyze this framing process in detail, let us lookat two simple examples of law: 1) the Pythagorean theorem; and 2) Fick's law of diffusion.

The Pythagorean theorem states that the length of the long side of a right triangle can be determined by the lengths of its two shorter sides. This relationship can be represented in algebraic form as...

$$a^2 + b^2 = c^2$$

When we declare that the Pythagorean theorem is a "law," we create the expectation that it will be found throughout nature. This means that we will frame nature in its terms. It also means that only those areas of nature that can be so framed will be considered. As Eddington said, "The mind imposes its demands by refusing toadmit any system of analysis... which does not yield parts with the required qualities." [100]

The framing utility of the "triangle" metaphor is so great that it spawned the school of geometry called trigonometry. Any area of possibility that can be grasped with this pattern of intention is contrived as finding a triangle therein, thereby unifying a large sector of possibility under one rubric.

Similar to the framing effect of the Pythagorean theorem is Fick's "law of diffusion." This law originated from the need to describe the combining of free particles between two chambers. The change in the concentration of the freely-moving particles when the two chambersare mixed is predicted by this law.

For instance, this law is used in medicine to measure "cardiac output" by sampling and comparing the concentration of oxygen atoms in the blood before and after its mixing while passing through in the heart.

Fick's "law of diffusion" can be represented algebraically as...

$$a = b\,(c/d)$$

This law can be stated as: "the rate of the diffusion of particles between two chambers is proportional to the difference in concentration between the two chambers." The variable "a" refers to the final concentration of the particles in the mixed chamber, the variable "b" is the rate of diffusion between the two chambers, and "c/d" is the initial concentration ratio between the two chambers. This law has been found to be useful for framing other areas of possibility where the investigator intuits a similar trajectory of intention. For instance, one can use it to predict the conduction of heat between two chambers, or the change in electrical voltage between two conductive systems. It even has been used to predict the pattern of migrating populations.

This act of "finding" Fick's law in such diverse areas seems almost magical. One would seem to have discovered a feature of reality in itself – that is, a law of nature. Upon reflection, one realizes that what appears as discovery in each instance is in fact the process of construing different areas of possibility in terms of this same metaphor. As Eddington said, the fundamental laws of nature "are all imposed by the human mind in this way, and are therefore wholly subjective." [101]

In the next chapter we will consider how the reduction of these laws to algebraic form helps in their extrapolation to multiple areas of possibility.

The *formative* metaphor function

With each instance of perception of possibility there emerges a new condition of existence for the subject. This is because the subject is the perceiver of possibility, such that the subject's anticipated and actual response to possibility is a formative act.

Through its response, the subject becomes more or less of what she has it in her to be as perceiver of possibility. As Emerson said, "in the soul of man there is a Justice whose retributions are instant and entire." [119] The subject may grow in its essential nature as perceiver of possibility, for instance in terms of its powers of perception and strength of character as an agent of response. Or it might wither in these by lack of responsive action.

The origin of the moral sense

This awareness of the potential of becoming is the origin of the moral sense. It is felt by the subject as a formative consequence of thought and action. It represents either the hopeful premonition of "participation in the universal or divine act of self-affirmation" as Tillich put it [126], or of grief over loss of substance to the self.

The sense of duty, that is itself the foundation of moral action according to Kant, is simply awareness of one's nature as perceiver of possibility. To respond to a sense of duty means to act consistent with one's essential nature as perceiver of possibility. In this sense the morally good is simply that which the "good" human-as-human does, as argued by Aristotle.

The subject may choose to respond affirmatively to her sense of responsibility to possibility, or to turn away from responsibility out of fear or of lassitude. But the choice itself is unavoidable. Both the moral decision and its effect on the subject are indelible.

This is the imperative feature of morality. Sartre

gives the example of being mobilized in war. One can choose to stay and fight or to desert. Either, in its own way, is a function of courage or of cowardice. One cannot hide behind circumstance to absolve oneself of this choice. It is the necessity of the choice, not the path chosen, that creates the moral condition. [120]

If the subject responds to the sense of responsibility, she acts with "integrity," as this is consistent with her nature as perceiver of possibility. On the other hand, if she turns away, by denying the choice, this effects a diminution of her being.

This diminution is perceived as a loss at a cosmic level because individual consciousness knows itself as a manifestation of the universe. This is why even a simple immoral act is characterized by a peculiar sense of grief. The weight of the moral decision thereby motivates us, as it goes to the heart of what we are.

Viktor Frankl gives an example of this compulsory aspect of the moral sense in his account of an interaction with a Nazis concentration camp guard. The guard mistook Frankl, being a physician, as coming from a privileged background and thus worthy of abuse. When Frankl revealed to him that he had done most of his work in clinics for the poor, the guard "threw himself on me and knocked me down, shouting like a madman." [121]

Acknowledging the moral sense with metaphor

Every objective formulation has a moral dimension, merely by virtue of its evocation of awareness of possibility. By virtue of this awareness alone one is made aware also of responsibility. But an objective formulation can be made into a moral proposition, per se, by formulating it so that it poses the question ofresponsibility directly.

This is accomplished by the use of terms such as "should" or "ought." The peculiar feature of these terms is that they combine the notion of obligation with the future tense, and in so doing pose the condition of responsibility for possibility.

For instance, the proposition, "One can be kind to others," is turned into an explicitly moral proposition with, "One should be kind to others." The power of the well-formed moral proposition lies in combining evoked perception of possibility with the proposition of the subject's responsibility for it.

Moral persuasion in evoked perception

Because the moral act is a response to possibility as it is perceived, rather than to specific possibility, there is an inherent ambiguity in all moral considerations.

A moral proposition need not coerce the subject with logical necessity, for the perception of possibility itself will carry the force of persuasion. If the moral proposition does not precipitate a sense of consequence, it will carry no moral weight, regardless of the philosophical or logical weight of its argument. The logical argument serves merely to precipitate awareness of consequential possibility, and thereby to evoke the moral sense.

The purpose of the moral proposition therefore is to precipitate perception of consequential possibility, and in terms that implicate the actor's responsibility. Various formulations rate as more or less morally powerful by the degree to which they precipitate this awareness. This is the creative work of the moralist.

An example in medicine is the difficult question of elective abortion. The statement that "abortion kills a life" precipitates a perception of possibility that is deep in its ramifications. This is because "life" is a term that we apply to our perception of the deepest manifestation of possibility. Therefore, it precipitates the deepest sense of responsibility.

But the question of abortion does not entail only the cessation of the life of the fetus. There is the human possibility to be explored in the question of the quality of life of a term birth, and the quality of the life of the mother. The moral actor has responsibility for these ends as well, by virtue merely of knowing of them.

As the psychoanalyst Magna Denes said in her account of her observations in an abortion clinic, there is no way to deny that abortion is a type of murder; but there also "is no way to say that it would not be just as surely murder, more cold and vengeful, to force little Flo to give birth to her bastard." [122]

One might defend the life of the fetus or of the mother. The moral persuasion, the sense of which choice is "less bad," will emerge from the relative weight of the perceived possibility. This persuasion will follow from the effectiveness of the moral argument in precipitating this awareness. What the physician needs from the moralist therefore is not the "right" moral code, but the formulation of moral code that elicits deeper perception of possibility.

The *reconciliation* metaphor function

The artificial split between subject and object in mind that is characteristic of consciousness causes the subject to become estranged from its ground in possibility. This is because the purpose of the split is to redirect the attention of the subject away from direct apprehension of the domain of possibility in which she partakes, and toward the object instead as the means of grasping this possibility.

The subject may retain a sense of her participation in the cosmic domain of possibility. As Tennyson said, she many know that she is "born to other things." But she is able to see in mind only the material object as the given agenda of thought. This limited view leaves her with the question, "Why am I here?" In other words, what is it to which the subject is essentially drawn, and for what purpose?

To address this need for reconciliation, the mind invokes a special kind of metaphor and metaphor induction that serves as a counterbalance to the Cartesiandualistic frame.

In this case a root metaphor is applied to grasp perception of the domain of possibility in its entirety, and specifically in a form with which the subject can interact for reconciliation.

This metaphorical grasp of the entire domain of possibility takes various forms, such as the Hindu "Brahman" or the Buddhist "Dharma" or the Chinese "Tao" or the personal "God" of the monotheistic religions, or the naturalistic universe of Spinoza. It is not mere coincidence that all of these metaphors pertain to a religious tradition; for what we call a religious tradition is simply the attempt to accommodate the subject's sense of her origin and role in the primal domain of possibility.(Religion: *religare* - to put things back together again.)

This application of metaphor is essential for the reconciliation of the subject to its ground in possibility. As Voltaire famously said, "If God did not exist, it would be necessary to invent him."

What is called God

Of course, Voltaire's proposition was intended to suggest that the psychic need of God renders authentic religious belief dubious. Possibility theory, on the other hand, looks upon this psychic need as the meaning of the notion of God and of similar attempts to grasp this primal domain. The question for us, then, is not whether God "exists" but what does God "mean."

In terms of each of the reconciling root metaphors above, the entire domain of possibility is projected as an object apart-from the subject in mind, and in a form withwhich the subject can interact.

Through the resulting subject-object interaction, the subject seeks to reconcile herself to the domain of possibility (what Tillich called the ground of being), of which she knows herself to be a manifestation, so to reorient her behavior, thoughts, and expectations with regard to this source that defines her.

Each metaphor supplies its own peculiar set of

categories in terms of which the subject works out this interaction. For instance, if the domain of possibility is contrived as a "personal God," as in the monotheistic traditions, this interaction might take the form of an effort at inter-personal communication, such as prayers of petition, supplication, intercession or worship.

Through such prayers, the universe reconciles itself to itself through the individual consciousness of the knowing subject. As the Christian mythology says, "Godwas in Christ, reconciling himself to the world."

Similarly, if the metaphor takes the form of a dynamic creative force, such as Brahman, the subject- object reconciliation may manifest as the subject's acquiescence to its identity as an expression of this universal principle. As Ryuichi Abe said in his introduction to the Buddhist text, *The Awakening of Faith*, individual consciousness "represents the Absolute as it is expressed in the temporal order." [124] Conversely, in the case of the naturalistic god of Spinoza or the static principle of the Chinese Tao, reconciliation of the subject might manifest as fidelity to a non- personal cosmic structure.

God experienced as possibility

As in all the other areas of subject-object interaction through metaphor induction at which we have looked, the domain of possibility gradually will reveal its nature through this dialectical interaction. The description of this nature develops in terms of the categories of the chosen root metaphor.

For instance, a personal God may be found to be "just" or "loving" or "demanding;" or Brahman may be found to "subsist within" all of reality; or the Universe may be understood by modern science to manifest in the mathematical laws of nature. In each of these cases the characteristics or manifestation of the divine realm will evolve toward its nature as open-ended possibility.

But here, in the case of the divine, there is an important difference from other instances of metaphor induction at which we have looked.

As the metaphor of the divine refers to the domain of possibility, interaction with the myth of God exists entirely at the level of possibility. As Tillich said, "everything divine transcends the split between potentiality and actuality." [189]

This places the notion of the divine in conflict with the hypnotic feature of metaphor induction, that posits all objects, including God, as a discoverable actuality in the world.

This creates a problematic dynamic between faith and lived experience, since the actual features of the world, such as suffering, are felt to be inconsistent with the intuited characteristics of God, such as love. This problem was referred to by Leibniz as the "theodicy."

The expectation of the actuality of features of the divine in the world, manifesting as the pervasive sense of "providence," creates the conditions for existential frustration, even resentment. Even Sarte himself at the end of his life confessed to Simone a feeling of cosmic purpose with reference to, while at odds with, his atheistic philosophical agenda...

Even if one does not believe in God, there are elements of the idea of God that remain in us and that cause us to see the world with some divine aspects... I don't see myself as so much dust that has appeared in the world, but as a being that was expected, prefigured, called forth. In short, as a being that could, it seems, come only from a creator; and this idea of a creating hand that created me refers me back to God... it is there, floatingvaguely. [204]

Seen from the perspective of possibility theory, faith is an affirmation of possibility, deeper than, and as the foundation of, actuality, but not dependent upon it. Therefore, the sense of "providence," as our relation to the domain of possibility, must be recast in terms of the Stoic notion of the courage to live with uncertainty regarding actuality.

The myth of discovery

Having introduced possibility theory, and metaphor induction, as they manifest in scientific, social, and medical decision making, a final task remains for us.

We must create a window to awareness on the part of the decision maker that the objective decision, in that it appears "given" as the end in itself, is thereby serving an end beyond itself in the grasp and actualization of human possibility. That is, we must show how the "discovery" language of objective science functions as a myth for the decision maker. Therein we can close the loop between the art and the science of medicine.

CHAPTER IV:
THE DISCOVERY MYTH

"In order to identify the myths of one's own culture, therefore, it is sufficient to ask: 'What constitutes my culture's sense of reality?'" [127]

-Michael Novak, The Experience of Nothingness

The necessity of myth

It has been our task up to now to explain how an evidence-based medical decision begins as a creative response to perception of possibility, as it is directly apprehended in the doctor-patient relationship. The hope is to establish that the objective decision depends upon subjective input from the doctor-patient interaction, and thereby to support the doctor in her inclination to return to the patient bedside.

As we saw in the last chapter, this creative process proceeds through the projection of metaphor onto possibility, to grasp it as an object for the subject. This precipitates the subject-object interaction whereby possibility, as the common ground of subject and object, is actualized.

We noted that the challenge to "discover" precipitates this creative response. That is, it functions as a myth to prompt the creative act of the decision maker.

It might seem sufficient therefore merely to alter the language of the medical decision, so that we refer to "applying metaphor," rather than to "discovering objects," and thereby to orient the decision maker to the creative origin of the objective decision.

But this will not do. The product of the medical decision does not appear to the user as a metaphorical grasp of possibility, but as the grasped possibility itself.

It appears discovered, not created. Only in this way does it precipitate the subject-object interaction whereby possibility is actualized, and that is the goal of the medical decision. As Paul Tillich said, a myth that is perceived as a myth "is for that very reason repelled." [9] So, for instance, a physician treating a patient's viral infection with the cognitive tools of immunology may conceive of a patient's white blood cells as "recognizing an invading virus as foreign" by its "histo-compatible" surface proteins. These terms will appear to her as the beginning and the end of the process. No thought need be given to their anthropic and metaphorical origin.

What we need to show is that, in appearing "discovered," this objective language is serving an end beyond itself in the grasp and actualization of human possibility. That is, it is serving as a myth.

To call a language system a "myth" is not to pass judgement on its truth or falsehood. It is to focus on the function that it serves for the user. Understanding this, the user can benefit from the language of discovery while appreciating that, in that it appears as the end-in- itself, it is serving an end beyond itself. In this way the user can benefit from the scientific rigor that an evidence-based approach affords, while understanding its relationship to the art of medicine.

We will look at the language of discovery and many of its associated notions, such as "reality," "law," "truth," "logic," "value," "duality," "time," "morality," and the "divine," each as they have evolved to facilitate the creative features of metaphor induction, as they pertain to medical decision making, and to the agenda of medicine as a social institution.

The mythological function of "reality"

The notion of "reality" follows as an adjunct of "discovery." It emerges from the presumption of a repository domain where objects are hypostatized as existing ahead of time, and wherein they are to be "found." This sets up and facilitates the creative flow of metaphor induction.

Eddington pointed out that, "The external world is the world that confronts that experience which we all have in common." [138] That is, the universe, as the common source of all individual consciousness, is experienced as a domain that is external to the mind. Therefore, it lends itself to being conceived of as a repository domain, that we call "reality." As Eddington said, "a very deep-rooted form of thought is that which formulates the knowledge acquired by observation as a description of a world." [130]

The myth of reality functions in the following way: We attribute characteristics to this domain of reality ahead of time, calling it the "nature of reality." Thereby, the objects that are created in terms of being "found therein" take on these same characteristics. Thus, the discovery myth begins by asking the question, "What is the nature of reality?" The notion of a discoverable reality thereby serves as a scaffolding for the ad hoc formulation of objects for the subject.

As the Nobel laureate physicist Frank Wilczek said, the basic question is, "What is the world made of?" We select notions such as the "ether" or "space-time" or the "quantum field" or a "gravitational grid." [140] For example, when Bertrand Russell begins his philosophical investigation by asking "How do we know about the physical world?" [131], he is setting the stage by begging the question of a "physical" reality in terms of which the world will be discovered.

Our modern cosmology, in its most basic form, is what Nagel calls a "naturalistic program," that proposes that "everything in the world is physical and that everything that happens in the world has its most basic explanation... in physical law." [141] Therein a physical nature is attributed to reality ahead of time.

Supplementing this, as we saw earlier, Eddington identifies several forms of thought that are reified into the domain of reality. For instance, we conceive of all of knowledge as a "description of a universe." This universe is presumed to be reducible to "a coexistence of a number of parts," taking the form of, for instance, the atomic concept, "such that the ultimate parts are identical structural units." This implies the "self-sufficiency of the parts" and their participation in a state of permanence that is conceived of as "substance." [142] Likewise, when we assume that reality is "logical" or "atomic" or "moral" in nature, the objects that we create in terms of "finding" them within this reality assume these characteristics. Therein lies the mythological function of the notion of reality.

The myth of health versus illness

The cosmology of an era presumes to describe the basic elements of reality. Any field of study undertaken during that era will begin with these cosmological features as its basic elements. Thus, in each era, "health" is ideally reified human possibility defined in terms of the cosmology of that era.

For instance, in Hippocrates' treatise, *On the Nature of Man*, his medical students were taught to conceive of health as a state of the "balance" of the four humors of the body (blood, phlegm, yellow bile, black bile), corresponding to the four elements of nature (earth, water, wind, fire). [26] The framework of the "balance of bodily humors" served as the scaffolding upon which hisstudents grasped human possibility.

This notion of health and of illness as a "balance" and an "imbalance" of humors persisted for hundreds of years, nurtured by the vast writing of the second-century Greek-Roman physician, Galen.

Even by the 18th century the notion of humoral balance contributed to medical care in the form of practices such as the bleeding of sick persons to remove excess blood, or cupping (applying hot cups to the skin) to remove excess bile, or the administration of emetic purges. Similarly, herbs and foods were prescribed basedon the notion of humoral balance, such that, for instance,a febrile and sweating patient might be given a cold and dry substance to eat.

This humoral-balance metaphor existed alongside an emerging notion of disease newly localizable instead to the various organs of the body, driven in part again by Galen and a new focus on animal dissection and comparative anatomy.

In the era of Robert Hook, with the benefit of the new tool of the microscope, the biological world came to be understood as a network of constituent cells. The botanist Henri Dutrochet proposed that the "cell" was the ultimate locus of health and illness, stating that it constitutes "the basic unit of the organized state." [27] So health and illness increasingly were conceived of in terms of the communication or failure thereof between these newly-identified units of the body. This comes down to our time in the form of the study of physiologic pathways between cells, such as hematology, neurology, endocrinology, and immunology.

With the emerging paradigm of molecular biology, health and illness increasingly are conceived of as "phenotypic" manifestations of an evolved or drifting wild-type, or a mutated genome, and the interaction of the resulting molecular products of the DNA code.

Illness in each era is described in the same terms as is health - but in the negative. Thus, for instance, Hippocrates posited illness as an "im-balance" of bodily humors. Today we posit illness as a disruption of physiological pathways, and increasingly as the aberrant interactions of protein products of mutated genes. By grasping human possibility in the negative as "illness," the mind is directed toward its actualization as "health," using the cosmological terms of the era as tools of actualization. This is the mythic utility of "health versus illness."

Cosmology thereby serves an ad-hoc heuristic role. For instance, Hippocrates did not doubt the existence of a discoverable "imbalance" prior to finding it in a case of illness. His cosmology told him that these were the elements of the universe, and therefore necessarily of human health and illness as well. This presumption of an imbalance served to set the metaphorical framework for the formulation of illness in terms of its discovery. The creative grasp of possibility thus took place in terms of the sequential steps of "finding the imbalance."

Similarly, today we do not doubt the existence of an entity of "disease" in an ill patient before searching for this disease entity. This assumption is valid, not because a disease entity has been demonstrated beforehand, but because the notion of a discoverable "disease" serves as the ad hoc framework upon which formulation of an illness is developed.

For instance, if one posits the existence of an "autoimmune disease" to explain a new dermatologic, renal, muscular or neurologic symptom in a patient, the theoretical edifice, that emerges in terms of "finding" the disease, will assume an immune molecular paradigm. Similarly, if one posits the existence of an infectious disease, the formulation will develop in terms of the stigmata of an invading organism. If one posits cancer, illness will develop in terms of the uncontrolled growth of a cell line. If one posits an endocrine disease, the description of the illness will develop in terms of underactivity or over-activity of a molecular hormone.

The goal, in the end, is not to find the correct diagnosis, but to develop an objective formulation, *in terms of* finding the correct diagnosis, for the grasp of human possibility in the negative.

The abiding myth of "health versus illness" thereby serves to support a continuous lineage for medicine despite the passing of discontinuous cosmologies.

Positing anthropic features into reality

The natural scientist and the clinical researcher posit into the domain of reality metaphors that serve to accommodate the contingencies of knowing as they are intuited. As Eddington said, these characteristics are "discovered a posteriori by physicists who employ that frame of thought, when they have come to examine the knowledge they have forced into it." [139] Thereby thereis laid down the anthropic foundation for creating well- formed objects for the subject.

As an example, Eddington says of the notion of the wave in physics that "we are as it were making our adopted basis of a priori probability a constituent of the world-structure - adding to the world a kind of symbolic texture." [87] In this constitutive act, "in the new physicsthe so-called probabilities are actually the real entities - the elemental stuff of the physical universe." [137]

Similarly, for example, an inherently perspectival notion of "symmetry" is taken to be a fundamental feature of the discoverable world in physics. As Capra said, the resulting discovery of symmetry led physicists "to believe that these patterns reflect the fundamental laws of nature." [143]

Of course, this does not mean that the "wave" or that "symmetry" are artificial or false; for in that the knower herself is a feature of the universe, the contingencies of knowing represent aspects of the nature of the universe itself.

Similarly, the notion of "locality" is introduced as a discoverable feature of the physical world. The anthropic notion of locality is confounded by the phenomenon of entanglement, wherein, as the science historian James Holt has said, "things that seem to be far apart may, at a deeper level of reality, not be truly separate at all." [144] This accommodates the brain's evolved pattern ofchanneling the self-perception of the universe into a form of objects separated in terms of space.

The dialectical nature of discovery

The emerging objective formulation grows in a dialectical fashion. As features of possibility are grasped in terms of categories of an applied root metaphor, the infinite nature of possibility resists these finite constraints. This prompts theoretical revision of the emerging object. This is contrived in terms of an ongoing, more exacting, "discovery" of the object.

Ongoing "discovery" are the terms in which possibility is better grasped by the evolving formulation. The object evolves to better reflect the nature of possibility only indirectly, however - that is, as a better-formed object for the subject.

For example, in his *Scientific Autobiography*, Max Plank recounted the creative process that "actually happened" when the metaphor of the material point came up against the quantum nature of reality. The notion of the point "had to be deprived of its basic, elementary character," giving way to the notion of waves, that "constitute the primary elements of the new world picture." The geometric point emerged intact as a specialcondition of the wave. [134]

This dynamic relationship between a formulated object and possibility is witnessed more transparently in the subjective medical sciences, such as psychiatry. In psychiatry, therapy progresses as its facts evolve based on their meaning to the patient and to the doctor. Therein, the "therapeutic truth" is a dialectical "creation of the relationship itself." [28]

But this creative process is no less immanent in the physical sciences and in medicine, though the subjective hand of the clinician is less apparent. For instance, the 20th-century polymath, Michael Polanyi, described his experience of an "existential choice" at the root of scientific discovery...

My account of scientific discovery describes an existential choice. We start the pursuit of discovery by pouring ourselves into the subsidiary elements of a problem and we continue to spill ourselves into further clues as we advance further, so that we arrive at discovery fully committed to it as an aspect of reality... To this extent, then, "existence precedes essence," that is it comes before the truth that we establish and make our own. [29]

The trajectory of the clinician's intention regarding perceived possibility is decisive in what will count as data. Data become the objects with which the clinician will interact, and thus whereby possibility is grasped. In this manner, as Polanyi says, we "establish the truth" andmake it our own.

The history of science manifests as a growing fabric of metaphors. Just as the metaphors of "point" and "line" were foundational to Euclid's formal system of geometry, and the "lever" and "force" basic to Newtonian physics, and the "field" and the "wave" basic to relativity and quantum theory, so are diagnostic metaphors, such as "immunity," "infection," "neoplasm," "histocompatibility," and "nerve conduction" elemental to medical practice.

These metaphors are rich with categories that provide the terms of data, causation, measurement, and the organizing axioms for constructing logical coherenceand formal proof.

This means that the scientist does not know the full nature of the objects of reality, such as the "atom" or the "gene," from the beginning. Kant argued that scientific knowledge grows through a dialectical process. The perceiver encounters reality through the products of the investigation itself, creating an ongoing "hermeneuticcircle," as Heidegger called it.

That is, in the attempt to actualize possibility through the application of metaphor, possibility pushes back against the limitations of the applied metaphor at each stage. Thereby possibility reveals its nature indirectly.

The response is a metaphorical revision of the object, conceived of mythologically as a deeper revelation of the object itself. As Marcus Aurelius divined poetically, the mind "makes the opposition which it encounters into material for itself." [41]

The metaphorical evolution of the "atom"

The basic form of objects posited into the repository domain of reality are construed to contain anthropic features. In this seminal form they persist throughout their development over time to maintain this anthropic utility.

For example, regarding the metaphor of the "atom," no commitment is made to its nature beyond the basic references to "size" and "divisibility" that already are inherent in the core notion. So, one might ask how Democritus could know in 400 BC that atoms exist as fundamental units of physical reality, and with the characteristics that he attributed to them, having never seen nor had experimental evidence of an atom.

Democritus' certainty arose from his intuition of the anthropic conditions of knowing that he posited into the basic form of the atom. The application of this root metaphor as fundamental to reality served to ensure that the grasp of possibility in terms of "finding an atomic structure" benefited from this basic anthropic rubric. Plato, writing just after Democritus, conceived of atoms as making up physical reality by assuming the shape of four of the five possible three-dimensional polyhedrons, and thereby accounting for the four basic substances of the world in physical terms:

fire, air, water and earth.

In the 19th century, prior to the notion of the atom as composed of a central nucleus surrounded by orbiting electrons, the chemist William Thomson (Lord Kelvin), seeking to explain chemical reactions in terms of atomic behavior, posited a "vortex" theory of the atom. In thishe imagined that the fundamental aether of space, described since Aristotle until the early 20th century as the medium of space, acts as a fluid that can form vortexes.

Lord Kelvin imagined these knotted tips of vortexes as stable, and so serving as the different atoms of observed chemical reactions. In this way, his theory evolved as an atomic hypothesis, adapting experimental findings to it. The current notion of atomic particles as manifestations of quantum fields harkens back to Lord Kelvin's notion of the atom.

Later in the early 20th century, Ernest Rutherford performed experiments with radiation, bombarding gold foil with helium nuclei. The observed pattern of scatter suggested the notion of deflection, presumed due to colliding particles, and was accommodated by his modification of atomic theory in which he introduced the notion of a central nucleus surrounded by empty space.

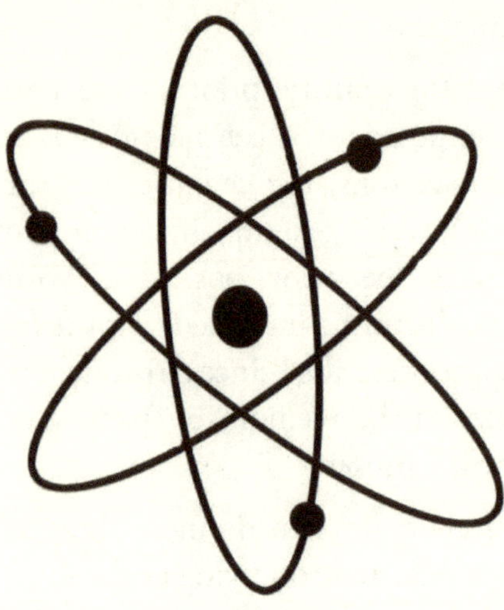

In so doing, in the words of Eddington, Rutherford rendered "concrete the nucleus which his scientific imagination had created." [42] Niels Bohr later brought this atomic model into line with quantum theory, introducing the notion of electrons as occupying energy shells around the nucleus.

In time, the "particle" manifested its conventional nature. As Planck described, the notion of the wave emerged to accommodate newly observed results, based upon, as Planck put it, whether the behavior of a moving electron is "studied through an electron microscope," or as refracted "through a crystal." [43]

This evolution of the theoretical object exposes its metaphorical utility in the service of an end beyond itself. As Niels Bohr said, the "isolated material particles are abstractions" whose properties are definable only interms of their manner of investigation. [44]

The similar evolution of the "gene"

As with the notion of the "atom," the "gene" was first posited only to accommodate certain anthropic needs of the knower in the study of heredity. The word "gene" itself was coined by the Danish botanist Wilhelm Johannssen in 1909. It was introduced simply as a unit vehicle of heredity, and thus as a means of tracking and investigating the mechanisms of heredity. Beyond this skeletal definition, Johannssen was non-committal as to the nature of the gene. As he said, "The word 'gene' is completely free from any hypothesis." [46] Thus, just as with the atom, the gene emerged to posit into reality certain anthropic preconditions of knowing.

One might ask how it is that Johanssen could proposeto know that an entity such as the gene existed before it had been demonstrated. Just as with the "atom" in physics, his positing of the "gene" emerged from an intuition of the anthropic needs of the knower. The gene was said to exist as a vehicle of heredity, so that it could be found and thereby contribute its anthropic features to the discovered mechanisms.

The positing of a reproducible unit of heredity set the stage for the eventual theoretical formulation of DNA as the molecular unit of heredity in 1953.

For centuries prior to this the positing and evolution of a vehicle of transmission required the application of various metaphors to serve as the notion of a vehicle of transmission. [45]

So, for instance, in 500 B.C. Pythagoras proposed the existence of "vapors" derived from the different organs of the body as the vehicle of heredity. He envisioned these vapors as uniting for the mixing of traits in the offspring. In the 17th century, following the microscopic discovery of cells, the Dutch biologist Jan Swammerdam posited the existence of specific "sex cells" in the body that contain "miniatures of the adult," to account for the passing of traits to offspring. In the 18th century, the mathematician philosopher Pierre Louis Maupertuis proposed the existence of "particles" from each bodypart that unite in sexual reproduction to pass on traits.

In the 19th century Charles Darwin improved upon the notion of particles, calling them "gemmules," and postulating that they originate in each body part and concentrate in the reproductive organs, so that offspring represent a "blending" of the parents' traits.

Gregory Mendel more pliably posited the existence of causal "factors," to account for his observation of the ratios of trait transmission in his botanical experiments. These factors correspond to what we now call genes.

Prior to the application of the metaphors of "code" and "molecule" to the notion of the gene, the physicist Erwin Schrodinger in 1943 sought to apply insights from quantum physics to the problem of heredity in his famous essay, "What Is Life?" Though Schrodinger was not a biologist, his work was acknowledged by Watson and Crick to have had an influence on their development of the DNA model.

Schrodinger's thought experiments introduced certain anthropic notions in an ad hoc manner necessary for the formulation of the molecular theory of DNA. Therein, Schrodinger sought to create for the biologist perspectival terms from which heredity could be explored. In this way he applied insights from quantum theory to the science of heredity, not in terms of quantum theory itself but through the creative path of theory development that quantum theory had demonstrated. That is, he worked backwards, from the form he felt the terms would have to take to accommodate the mind in its encounter with the phenomenon of heredity.

Schrodinger sought specifically to address the observation that chromosomes (by then seen with the microscope) contain only a relatively small number of atoms, yet appear able to transmit the entire pattern of anorganism in a regular fashion. To accommodate this, he suggested that the gene be presumed to have the nature both of a "molecule" and of a "code-script." [47]

The modern science of heredity developed in termsof the discovery of DNA through a formulation of the gene in terms of these notions. The notions of "code- script" and of "molecular" transmission appear to us now as merely obvious. But historically they were posited before their discovery. The theory of DNA as a molecular code-script took shape through the application of these anthropic terms, to guide the conditions of discovery.

Our argument here is not that these concepts do not represent the true nature of the gene, but that they accommodate the anthropic contingencies of knowing in their objective grasp of the possibilities inherent in the notion of heredity. In this way anthropic contingencies of knowing are introduced into the emerging objective theory of DNA.

Matthew Cobb, in his history of genetics theory [48], further explored the emergence of the notion of "coded information" in DNA theory in a way that underscores its conventional origin.

He pointed out that a molecular strand of RNA, emerging prior to DNA, can be envisioned to have been able to copy itself through simple atomic bonding. This self-copying process itself does not require the notion of "coded information." But, if one were to invoke the notion of "coded information" to describe this process, then the RNA strand can be said to have been "its own code." It is, as Cobb says, "a way of thinking about life in terms of flows of control and information, a way of thinking about how genes worked." [48] The notion of a "selfish gene" as the unit of heredity did not anticipate the higher-level process of real-time adaption to open- ended possibility that appears now as a basic mechanismof molecular biology.

The myth of "phenotype and genotype"

When we analyze the metaphorical construct of molecular biology, we see that it accommodates anthropic contingencies of knowing in its structure. This is represented in the notions of phenotype and genotype.

The genetic investigation of a specific disease begins with a description of the phenotype. This is true even though the genotype, that includes the genetic locus and its molecular products, is posited as the "cause" of the phenotype. Nevertheless, one begins with a description of the phenotype because this is where the subjective metaphorical grasp of open-ended possibility first occurs, apprehended directly in the doctor-patient encounter.

Any feature of life, any aspect of human possibility, is amenable to its objective grasp as a "trait" in terms of the phenotype by using a metaphor that accommodates the clinician's subjective impression. This might include a description of gender, race, eye color, body habitus, hair texture, intelligence, personality types, voice pattern, cancer risk, even consciousness itself.

In this way, the liberal metaphorical structure of the phenotype accommodates the open-ended nature of perceived possibility. Any metaphor will do if it is effective in grasping human possibility as it is perceived. This creative liberty afforded by the notion of the phenotype is part of the power of molecular biology as a tool for grasping and actualizing human possibility.

Phenotype and Genotype. *Susan Saandholland on Midjourney*

On the other hand, the "molecular" formulation of the genotype, presumed to be the cause of the phenotype, is bounded strictly by the terms of the root-metaphor of interactive molecules.

The positing of a causal genotype begins by naming the genetic locus after the already-formulated phenotype, even before the genotype is found. This sets the molecular formulation of the genotype, in terms of its discovery, on the path of grasping human possibilityfrom the perspective of the phenotype. This is why, for instance, one identifies a "dystrophin" gene as the sourceof the "dystrophin" protein in Duchenne muscular dystrophy, or why the gene that causes the childhood tumor "retinoblastoma" is called the "RB" gene.

The molecular metaphor of the genotype does not exist to grasp possibility as it is encountered, as does the phenotype. Instead, it serves the equally-important roleof creating a well-formed object for the subject. Themolecular metaphor creates an object that possesses anthropic handles, such as the uniform units of a molecule, that are important as the causal tools for grasping and actualizing intended possibility.

As the genotype is said to "account for" the phenotype, the formulation of its molecular causal link is accomplished in terms of its discovery. This means that causal links, defined in molecular terms, will be construed as proceeding from the genetic locus to the observed phenotype.

In this way, the molecular interactions of molecular biology play a role similar to the atoms of atomic theory. They are posited first into the nature of reality, so that in the process of discovering them there, the genotype assumes its anthropic form.

The goal of the investigation is stated as mapping the cause of the phenotype from the genetic locus. From the perspective of possibility theory, the goal is more utilitarian. It is the creation of a metaphorical formula, in terms of discovery, whereby human possibility can be grasped for its actualization. This perspective of molecular biology as myth leaves the clinician and the investigator aware of the deeper ground of possibility from which arises the medical decision.

As the molecular formulation develops in terms of its discovery, the limiting metaphorical boundaries of both the phenotype and the genotype make themselves known, requiring concessions on the part of each in deference to the other. Since the goal is to create a coherent causal link, the contingencies of locating illness within the genetic code requires this ongoing dialectical reformulation.

In some cases, a reformulation of the phenotype is necessary to accommodate the limits of the molecular metaphor of the genotype. In other cases, the molecular description of the genotype must bend to accommodate the phenotypic definition as it was originally formulated. Sometimes this molecular reformulation does not admit of a direct causal link from a singular genetic locus to an intended phenotypic description. In such cases the molecular formulation will invoke "epigenetic" features, such as variable penetrance and environmental forces. The definitions of the phenotype and of the genotype will be reworked until the causal link emerges. When multiple genetic loci are found to result in the same subjective phenotype, a condition known as "genetic heterogenicity" is said to exist. This term belies the primacy of the phenotypic impression. An example of this is the bleeding disorder called "hemophilia," thatis associated with mutations at either of two loci on theX chromosome, one leading to a deficiency of factor VIII (hemophilia A) and the other to a deficiency of factor IX (hemophilia B).

Another example is the disease entity named "hereditary hemorrhagic telangiectasia," that manifests phenotypically as multiple arterial-venous malformations throughout the gastrointestinal track, the lungs and the brain. It has been found to be associated with mutations of either of two genes, one on chromosome 9, or another on chromosome 12. The manifestation of this disease, of either genetic locus, varies widely between individuals, requiring the positingof additional unknown epigenetic factors. [32]

Most hereditary diseases, when carefully analyzed, prove to be genetically heterogeneous. [105] This underscores that, just as what we call "equal" refers to perspective, so what we call "disease" is a function of perspective.

The pliable phenotype serves to keep the formulation true to the clinician's apprehension of possibility. The genotype appropriates the utility of its molecular model to ensure the emergence of a well-formed anthropic object for the subject. The final formulation is a composite compromise between these two.

Describing cancer in terms of the molecular myth

As an example of this creative process, the task of describing cancer within a genetic framework requires an ad hoc positing of two classes of genes: "oncogenes" that arise by mutation and that promote tumor growth; and "tumor suppressor genes," that normally limit cell growth, so that malignant cell growth can be attributedto their mutation. [147]

One describes the molecular path to a manifesting cancer in terms of finding these genes. These loci are notfound ahead of time, leading to a genetic theory of cancer. Instead, they are required by the contingencies offormulating a cause of cancer in terms of molecular interaction.

For instance, consider the disease named "retinoblastoma," that is a cancer of the eye that emergesby age 5 in roughly one in every 20,000 births. It has been traced to a genetic source: a mutation of the RB (for retinoblastoma) gene on chromosome 13.

This RB gene is said to be a "tumor suppressor" gene. This means that in its normal state the product of this gene acts to "prevent" an uncontrolled growth of retinal cells. If the normal RB gene is not there (due to a mutation), then an uncontrolled growth of retinal cells results. Thus the gene is said to exist as a "tumor suppressor gene" in that its removal by mutation results in abnormal cell growth.

So, we see that formulating a molecular theory of cancer begins by positing a "suppressor" class of gene, whose suppressor function is disrupted by its mutation. We then create a causal link in molecular terms by "finding" these oncogenes as mutated tumor-suppressor genes within the genome.

To appreciate the ad hoc nature of this process, it is helpful to consider that the necessity of positing a suppressor gene emerges because disease requires illness to be a deviation from a normal state. Thus, we posit a normal gene whose existence serves to hold the illness atbay. It is a "suppressor" gene by virtue of the fact that one can account for the illness by its absence.

By extension, any gene can be said in some way to bea "suppressor" of the illness that would result from its mutation. By first naming it a "suppressor" gene, we set the anthropic conditions for describing a molecular link from genome to phenotype. This does not mean that the suppressor gene "does not really exist." It means that its existence as a suppressor gene is a function of the perspective of the clinician.

The myth of natural selection

To appreciate the influence of the contingencies of knowing in the biologic sciences more broadly, let us consider the notion of "natural selection" as it functions as a myth for biological theory.

From the perspective of possibility theory, the process of evolution is the emergence of possibility into actuality in the biologic realm. Therefore it can be understood as rendering a natural teleology to the life sciences. All that emerges as life is a manifestation of possibility and of its nature.

In classical evolution theory, on the other hand, the only guiding principle considered inherent to the process of evolution is the combined effect of random variation and selection through competition, the so-called "survival of the fittest."

The notion of "random" in this instance implies the absence of a pre-determined pattern, and thus of no meaning. As Eddington said, "randomness is a negation of law." [56] Or as the physicist Paul Davies said regarding evolution theory, there is "no preordained 'best fit', no optimal adaptation, and no fixed 'goal' towards which natural selection steers evolution." [57] Therefore, we say that the inherent teleology of evolution renders "no meaning" to evolved life.

From the perspective of possibility theory, however, and put very simply, all of life, including consciousness, arises as a manifestation of possibility. It could not be otherwise. Possibility is an ontological precondition of all that is actual. The products of evolution manifest only because they are possible; and the random stochastic process at the molecular level serves to manifest possibility. Thereby, evolution manifests the nature of possibility itself, and so has the deepest of all possible meaning. It is not simply the persistence of mutated genetic products through natural selection.

The word "random" is perspectival. It means that one does not know the preconditions of the emerging actuality. What we call "natural selection" or "survival of the fittest," are the infinite conditions of possibility seen from the perspectival narrative of "competition" or "struggle." This is the myth of classical evolution. These are the terms with which we describe the products of evolution in a limited way as random ends in themselves, not as manifestations of possibility.

In reality, the conditions of evolution have a much more fundamental structure that we cannot see, the infinite boundaries of the domain of possibility.

Manifestation of possibility into actuality, not mere survival, is the process. So, the "natural" in natural selection is the nature of possibility itself. This process appears random to us because its possible manifestations are infinite. But this is a bounded infinity. That is, not everything is possible, meaning that evolution is the manifestation of a fundamental nature.

Considering randomness at the subatomic level, it has seemed probabilistically inconceivable that a product as complex as life, in that it requires exacting universal constants that must have been present or have come into being at the moment of the initial quantum fluctuations, could have arisen from a process that is inherently random. It would seem that there must have been insteada force or principle from without to guide the emergenceof these constants toward this end.

However, randomness is merely the manifestation of possibility. If all that is possible must occur in time, suchas every possible variation of the quantum fluctuations - for instance, those that create the carbon molecule and those that do not - as is posited in the multiple-universe theory in physics, then random variation simply secures the inevitability of the carbon molecule, and of life as a manifestation of possibility.

Or, if possibility, by virtue of its bounded nature (theboundary conditions), selects out what manifests fromthe initial quantum perturbations, then it drives both the activity of the manifesting of actuality and the nature ofthe manifest actuality. This is a process that would not require the heritable variations of multiple universes, andwas described in Alan Turing's "metamorphosis" model(published in 1952, two years before his death, and oneyear before elaboration of the molecular model of DNA).

Paraphrasing that model, one can give the analogy of a bowl of water resting stagnant. The inner rim of the bowl sets the boundary conditions of interacting wave patterns set in motion by a single ripple on the water surface. The final pattern of ripples is determined by the boundary conditions fixed by the rim of the bowl.

Possibility therefore is the teleological meaning of life. Not only is life not meaningless, it must be said to carry the deepest meaning as possibility manifesting.

The myth of value judgment

A special problem arises for the classical myth of evolution with regard to the notion of value judgments. Classical evolution theory assumes that the products of evolution are random and therefore are without meaning. But consciousness has evolved as a search for standards that can stand on their own, and upon which one can make value judgments regarding truth, beauty, morality, aesthetics, etc.

From the perspective of classical evolution theory this search for independently-valid standards would seem to be an illusion or a false hope. As Thomas Nagel pointed out, if the faculties that generate our value judgments are the result of natural selection, then the contents of consciousness would appear to suffer from the same meaninglessness. [58]

For there to be valid value judgments, either there must be an external, supra-natural source of their origin, or the soup from which consciousness arises must itself render a meaningful teleology to both consciousness and its content. It is this latter condition that we find in the natural teleology of possibility theory.

That is, consciousness is both manifest possibility and the perceiver of possibility. Therefore, it can be understood as reaching into its own source, into possibility itself, for meaning. When one seeks for objective truths in science, one is seeking for what is possible; when one seeks for moral truths, one is asking about responsibility to perceived possibility; when one finds beauty, one is recognizing the manifesting of possibility. As the physicist Steven Weinberg surmised, the sense of beauty in physics, as in music, is the impression of inevitability.

Sartre described human consciousness as a process of the mind reaching beyond itself at any one time and into open-ended possibility...

Man is constantly outside of himself; in projecting himself, in losing himself outside of himself, he makes for man's existing; and on the other hand, it is by pursuing transcendent goals that he is able to exist;

man, being this state of passing-beyond, and seizing upon things only as they bear upon this passing-beyond, is at the heart, at the center of this passing-beyond. [201]

The notion of "pre-existing" value standards serves mythologically to facilitate the metaphorical grasp of open-ended possibility, that is the creation of standards in terms of discovering them. This myth is the notion of "value realism," described by Nagel as "moral and evaluative truths that do not depend on our own beliefs." [166]

This search for independent values is the heuristic edifice that guides the metaphorical grasp of the conditions of possibility.

The discovery myth seen historically

One can more-easily observe the emergence of the discovery myth historically. For example, as we considered earlier, Elizabeth Patterson, in her account of the origin of the atomic theory of chemistry in the 18th century, described the initial reservations with the atomic hypothesis as "a reluctance to accept as the 'elements of chemical combination' any metaphysical entities such as were atoms.'" [132] However, once the actions of various gases were explained by John Dalton in terms of their atomic weight, the atomic nature of chemistry appeared given as "discovered." It was from this impression of discovery that the myth of discovery itself developed.

Atomic Chemistry. *Susan Saandholland on Midjourney*

That is, Dalton extrapolated from his experience of the given appearance of the metaphorical product by proclaiming that the purpose of scientific knowledge in general is the "discovery of new and important facts; but much more when these facts lead to the establishment of general laws." [133]

In this we observe that the appearance of the product as "discovered" spawned and sustained the discovery myth itself. Thereby the challenge to "discover" promptsthe creative act of metaphor induction.

Similarly, we have discussed the dialectical nature whereby scientific knowledge grows through metaphor induction. Awareness of this dialectical nature threatens to expose the creative hand of the scientist and thereby threatens the integrity of the discovery myth. The myth has evolved to ward off this threat by the manner in which it refers to the ongoing creative process.

For instance, one does not refer to the dialectical process as the result of an "incomplete metaphorical grasp of possibility." Rather, one asserts that the scientist merely has come up short, in that her "observations" are not sufficiently rigorous. That is, the winding road of scientific discovery is said to reside not in the perspectival nature of scientific knowledge but in anincomplete perception of immovable objects. As Eddington said, we simply "can and do call the resulting observation a 'bad observation'." [135]

This preserves the hypnotic appearance of the object as discovered. The scientist is sent back to the drawing board, and the medical student back to the patient. One indicts the observer for a less-than-rigorous observation, rather than acknowledging the metaphorical and thusinherently incomplete nature of "observation" itself. The resulting reformulation takes place in terms of a more "rigorous observation" of the given object.

Similarly, the discovery myth handles the tectonic shift in root metaphor, that we discussed in the previous chapter as a "paradigm shift," simply with the claim that the objects populating a previous paradigm, such as elemental phlogiston or the universal ether or gravity as a force (in the traditional sense), simply never did really "exist." Thereby the myth of discovery itself is salvaged.

The limitations of positing a physical reality

As we have seen, the hypnotic feature of metaphor induction masks the metaphorical origin of the object. This results in a strict positivism that risks the denigration of other terms with which one might have more effectively grasped features of possibility.

For instance, the 20th century behavioral psychologist B.F. Skinner famously proposed that when describing behavior it is better to avoid "mentalistic terms," because the "mind is nothing more than a manifestation of physiology." This exclusively physical cosmology led him to discount terms such as "Herbert Spencer's 'life force,' or Schopenhauer's 'blind will to exist,' or Bergson's 'elan vital'" as a means of understanding human behavior. [145]

Even if it is true that a purely material (behavioral) psychology is preferable for practical reasons, it still is the case that what will be said to count as a "physical cause" or as an "objectively observed fact," or as the patient's "material environmental history," is ultimately a formulation derived in response to the apprehension of possibility perceived in the doctor-patient relationship. That is, avoiding non-material terms in deference to physical reductionism does not spare one from the creative imperative.

Furthermore, there may be features of human experience that are not amenable to the metaphorical boundaries of a "physical" cosmology. The physical does not represent the limits of the known, but the limits of knowing. The distinction between the medical decision as created versus discovered can be illustrated by looking at an early artifact of evidence-based medicine in the 20th century called "decision analysis."

Consider the decision tree below, that represents the clinical decision whether to treat carotid artery occlusion with surgery or with medication. Each decision node in this decision tree is shown with its expected outcomes weighted with their known probabilities and theirsubjective clinical utilities.

Taking this diagram to represent the medical decision, the clinician can review the objective elements of the decision. As constructed, the structure of the decision tree appears given as evidentiary "findings" anddata points that are independent of the clinician's input.

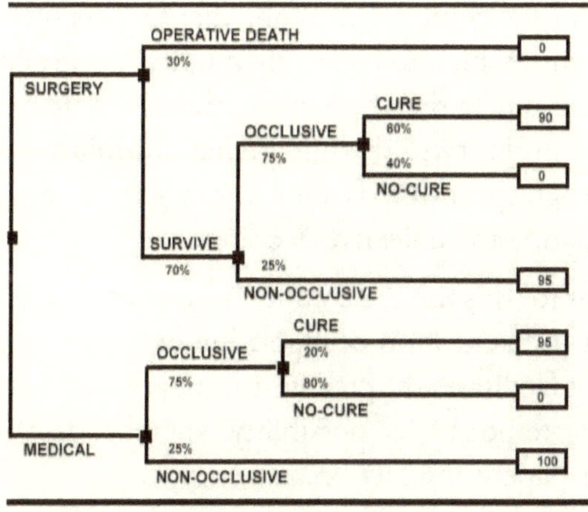

The decision tree thereby appears as an objective guide for the clinician. The necessary outcomes of its causal links, as calculated, appear to establish the necessary truth of the conclusion.

This illusion contributed to the creation of clinical computer decision tools in the late 20th century, into which the clinician was directed simply to type data based on prompts, and to passively receive output that was calculated based on stored probabilities. One presumes that a computer tool based on such an algorithm can feed the correct decision to the clinician. However, there are two ways to view this diagram:

One is to take its nodes to represent the decision pointsof the medical decision as given. The other is to see in this decision tree a display of the metaphorical terms with which clinical possibility is contrived as nodes that make up the moments of the decision.

This latter mythological perspective changes the tree diagram from a tool that makes the decision on behalf of the clinician, into one that renders the tree as a tool with which to creatively modify the structure of the decision. It thereby renders the clinician aware of herresponsibility to the underlying possibility that she seeksto grasp. In this fashion it can serve as a tool for formulating the objective decision.

But for this use the computer must be programmed with a different kind of algorithm and user interface, onethat facilitates the creative formulation of a decision tree in response to possibility apprehended in the doctor-patient interaction.

The mythology of natural law

As we saw in the last chapter, the notion of natural law comes into being when a common root metaphor is applied to multiple areas of perceived possibility where the same trajectory of intention can be made to apply. By accepting such laws as given, the subject is agreeing to structure the world within their finite terms.

We noted that there are different kinds of laws. There are those that apply to specific trajectories of intention, such as the Pythagorean theorem, and those that apply to all instances of knowledge because they grasp the contingencies of knowing itself. These latter are called the "laws of nature," for they can be made to applyanywhere nature will be described.

One such law of nature is Newton's first law of thermodynamics. This law of the "conservation of energy" was described by Eddington as emerging to accommodate the anthropic need for "permanence," formulated in terms of the "conservation of mass, or energy, or momentum, or electrical charge." [150]

In the 19th century the notion of entropy became part of the study of thermodynamics. It can be thought of as the measure of disorder in a closed system. Entropy exists necessarily as a function of the perspective of the user, since order, and so disorder, are inherently perspectival. The user will insert the notion of entropy into a physical formulation by deciding ahead of time what counts as a "closed system" - a closed system beingdefined as that in which energy, as order and disorder,are preserved.

In this way, the notion of entropy satisfies the anthropic need to define a system as a framework that permits a common basis of measurement. This is not to say that entropy does not exist, but that its existence is a function of the subject's perspective as the measuring entity.

The notion of "law" functions as myth when we posit these laws as existing within the nature of reality, then formulate objects as if "discovered" to be adhering to these laws. Thereby, they become the set of root metaphors through which all of possibility is organized.

As an example, we looked at how the metaphor of the triangle is used to grasp multiple areas where the same trajectory of intention can be made to apply, in terms of the Pythagorean theorem. Similarly, we looked at how the metaphor of the diffusion of particles between chambers, formulated as Fick's Law, can be made to apply to multiple areas of possibility, such as transfer theheat, electrical conduction, and population migration, in that these phenomena are amenable to this one trajectory of intention. Another example is the universalapplication of the method of calculus since its development by Newton and Leibniz.

Deriving Calculus. *Susan Saandholland on Midjourney*

This method at root is simply the formulation of diverse areas of possibility in terms of a common root metaphor. Any experience that is susceptible to analysis as a series of approximating intervals can, on that count, be reformulated geometrically as the area under a curve that is created by plotting these intervals as cartesian coordinates on a graph. Thus, everywhere calculus is applied, possibility is grasped as the area under a curve.

As David Hilbert famously said, in his *Axiomatic Thought* of 1918, "The art of mathematics is finding that special case that contains all the germs of generality."

That is, the art of mathematics lies in applying a root metaphor within whose parameters the features of possibility can be grasped on a broad scale.

We saw in the last chapter how the process of extrapolating metaphors to other areas of possibility is facilitated by their reduction to algebraic form. This reduction frees trajectory of intention from its metaphorical moorings. It permits the application of pure trajectory of intention to multiple areas of possibility, independent of the metaphor.

Consider the Pythagorean theorem. By replacing the sides of a triangle with variables (a, b and c), one reduces their definition to mere distinction from one another, so that their grasped intention relative to one another may be referred to in isolation. Then, by representing their intentionality relative to each other with number, the mind is freed to extrapolate not the metaphorical content itself (such as a "triangle"), but the interrelations of intention captured by the triangle.

Likewise, this reduction to pure intentionality occurs in Fick's law of diffusion by replacing "particles" and chambers with variables, then reducing their interactions to numerical relations. Thereby other areasof possibility as diverse as temperature change and population migration can be construed and formulated interms of these same intentional interactions.

That is, it is not the metaphor that is extrapolated. Rather, the extrapolated element is the trajectory of intention represented algebraically. For instance, this is why the rubric of "harmony" can be applied as an organizing notion to areas having nothing to do with musical sound. The mathematical form represents only the trajectory of intention as it was applied in the original metaphor. As Eddington said, the fundamental laws "are simply a mathematical formulation of the qualities of the parts into which our analysis has divided the universe." [151]

The algebraic reduction is successful because of the mind's capacity to extrapolate from one situation to another at the level of pure intentionality. When applying a law to other areas of possibility, the user uses the metaphor only as a reference for orientation.

This mathematical reduction of natural law became a hallmark of the scientific myth in the 16th century and coming to bloom with Newton. As Nagel said, Galileo and Descartes "made the crucial conceptual division by proposing that physical science should provide a mathematically precise quantitative description of an external reality." [153]

The myth of western science therein evolved to

posit a mathematical reality, wherein physical law was formulated as discovered therein. As Eddington said, "Small wonder then that physical science should have evolved a conception of the world consisting of entities rigorously bound to one another by mathematical equations forming a deterministic scheme." [152]

Intentionality as the origin of number

The need to refer to pure intentionality without regard to metaphor, is the origin of "number," and so of mathematics as the representation of number relations. That is, number refers to pure intentionality.

The foundation of number lies not in the chosen metaphor, such as a geometrical figure, or the intensity of sound, or the mass of an object, or the rate of acceleration. Its foundation lies in the intention regarding possibility harnessed by these metaphors. The "number" is a content-less formal representation of intention, stated in association with the manner of its measurement - such as the units of time, size, weight, speed, pattern, etc.

Similarly, the basic functions of mathematics, in that they refer to number, refer to intentionality. As Eddington proposed, mathematical symbols "represent elements of knowledge, not entities of the external world." [104] For instance, the function of equivalence represented by the equal sign "=" means that two objects are the same from the perspective of intentionality.

Number as Intentionality. *Susan Saandholland on Midjourney*

To say of two or more objects that they are "equal" is to say that they grasp the same intention regarding possibility, and in terms of number that they are "one" inthe same or "two of" the same, etc. Therefore, equality initself is not an inherent feature of possibility. It exists only at the level of intentionality relative to possibility. This is the mythological role of number. The process of enumerating is the designation of distinct manifestations of possibility as the same class of thing in terms ofintentionality.

Number did not begin as an abstract concept. Morris Kline describes the progression of number, from concrete application of metaphor, to pure self-referential abstraction. He describes how for the early Pythagoreans numbers referred to geometrical shapes. Thus, one spokeof "triangular numbers, square numbers, pentagonal numbers, and others... thinking of collections of points, pebbles, or point-like objects arranged in those shapes."[102]

From this was made an abstraction of number, probably required by and heralded by its application to itself, and so requiring an exclusive terminology, and so number as number.

Because of the hypnotic nature of metaphor induction, the application of a number, such as "three," appears to pertain not to grasped intention regarding possibility, but to itself only. It appears given as an end in itself. Thereby number appears to be an independent feature of the discoverable world, with no external referent. Its reference to intentionality remains occult.

In the manipulation of number, however, the mind responds tacitly to intentionality regarding possibility, without recognizing it as such. So, the mathematician has a sense of responding to a guiding principle that is singularly called "number," not cognizant of its source. As Bertrand Russell said, "mathematics may be defined as the subject in which we never know what we are talking about, nor whether what we are saying is true." [103]

The "laws of logic" as myth

As we saw in the last chapter, the categories of an applied root metaphor render coherence to an objective formulation in terms of the root metaphor, and are characterized as an internal logic. Specifically, the formulated findings appear to lead back to the root metaphor from which they are derived as their necessary conclusion.

For instance, in that a sophist is found to be a "hunter for tame animals at rivers of wealth," he appears necessarily to be an angler. In that cancer is found to arise from the "mutation of a tumor suppressor gene," it appears necessarily to be a genetic disease.

From the perspective of possibility theory, the utility of coherence lies in the causal links that it provides for the grasp and actualization of the intended possibility. From the naive perspective, however, its logical necessity appears simply as the necessary "truth" of the formulation itself.

This process of creating a coherent formulation from metaphor is facilitated by codifying the features of metaphor induction as they form this coherence, referring to them as the laws of logic - then positing them into reality, and so requiring that the emerging formulation follow their pattern. As Eddington said, "by consideration of certain deeply rooted forms of thought we can foresee the fundamental laws." [106]

The codified features of metaphor induction are thus conceived of as the "laws of logic." The discovery myth functions by positing these laws into the nature of reality, then requiring objective theory to adhere to them in their formulation.

Let us consider two examples of contingencies of metaphor induction as they are codified as laws of logic: the law of "excluded middle," and 2) the principle of "modus ponens." We will see that each law is actually a feature of metaphor induction that, when adhered to as ifit were a discoverable feature of reality, facilitates coherent metaphorical formulation.

The law of excluded middle can be represented formally as...

(A v ~A)

This can be stated as "either A or non-A." This simply means that one can apply a metaphor by stating iteither in the positive or in the negative, but not both at the same time. For instance, an object is either "hot" or "not hot," or a theoretical concept is either "intelligible" or "not intelligible," but not both at the same time. Thereby, a contingency of applying metaphor is stated asa law of logic, to which the emerging formulation is made to adhere.

As Nietzsche pointed out, this prohibition against affirming and denying the same thing at one time "is a subjective empirical law, not the expression of a 'necessity' but only of an inability." [107] That is, it pertains to all of reality because it an anthropic contingency of knowing.

Another law of logic that represents a contingency of metaphor induction is the rule of "modus ponens" (Latin for "mode that affirms"). This law is basic to all coherent systems. It can be stated this way: "if A impliesB, and if A is true (the condition designated as 'C'), then B is true." Its symbolic representation is...

$$A \rightarrow B) \wedge C \rightarrow I$$

From the perspective of metaphor induction, thislaw simply says that an applied category (A) implies a root metaphor (B) from which it is derived. For instance, if a patient's rash on biopsy is said to manifest "immune vasculitis" (A), this implies an "immune disease" (B). Thus, if an immune vasculitis is found (C) the patient must have an immune disease (B). It is therein a basic unit of coherence. From the perspective of the discovery myth, it signifies the "logical necessity" of the root metaphor, and therein its "necessary truth."

From the perspective of the discovery myth, logic appears to be a condition of scientific truth. Therefore, it became an important project of the 20th century to find and codify all laws of logic. As Geoffrey Hunter stated, the ultimate aim of logicians was to find "a system or set of systems that caught all truths of pure logic." [108]

The myth of formal logic

From the naive perspective of the discovery myth, the goal of logical coherence is simply to establish the truth of a formulation. Therefore, the act of creating coherence is called a "proof." The structural elements of a proof have been systematized as a "formal proof." The purpose of this formal tool, from a mythological perspective, is to guide the formulation of an argument into a form that establishes its truth.

The main constituent parts of a formal proof are its "axioms" and its "theorems." Each of these represents an essential feature of metaphor induction. An "axiom" is a root metaphor that provides the categories in terms of which findings are formulated. In medicine for example a "diagnosis" functions as an axiom. In terms of its categories a patient's symptoms will be described.

These construed findings, formally called "theorems," will appear to be "derived" from the axioms, as they are described in terms of the axioms.

This logical construct will take the form either of an "inductive" or a "deductive" proof. The difference lies in which of the elements one takes as given when forming the coherent structure: either the axioms (such as diagnoses) or the theorems (such as symptoms). We will see that, from the perspective of logical necessity, it makes a difference whether the proof is inductive or deductive.

For example, in Euclid's deductive system of geometry, the axiom of the "point" was considered to be given as true. Its truth was said to lie simply in that it exists undeniably as a feature of the world. One then formulated facts about the world, derived as theorems, interms of this axiom of the system. The assumed truth of the axioms of the deductive system, combined with the logical "necessity" of the derivation of theorems, was taken to establish the "necessary truth" of the formulation. For this reason, deductive proof was the preferred form of argument in science.

However, in contrast to this deductive system, most of the formal proofs in science, including in medicine, are inductive in form, not deductive. One begins with a finding, such as a symptom or a test result. Then one attempts to establish its logical necessity by finding an axiom or axioms in terms of which to describe it as a "derived" theorem.

For instance, a patient might present to a doctor with a red and tender rash on her arms and legs.

The physician knows that this rash might be said to be caused by any number of diagnoses. Based on its association with other symptoms in this patient, the doctor might propose that the patient has, for example, systemic lupus erythematosus (SLE).

Since SLE is an autoimmune disease, the doctor will seek to establish this diagnosis as an axiom by finding other stigmata of an autoimmune process in this patient, such as abnormal auto-antibodies in the patient's blood. If these are found, then an evidence-based proof can be constructed that implicates the rash as an autoimmune vasculitis linked to SLE. The rash can be said therefore to be proven, by inductive reasoning, to bean autoimmune vasculitis.

The physician knows that the rash might be an autoimmune vasculitis caused by SLE. But she knows that there are other possible diagnostic causes of a rash, such as a viral exanthem, or an infection such as Rocky Mountain Spotted Fever, or the vascular flair of hormonal over-activity as in pheochromocytoma, or the embolic phenomena of endocarditis, or dermal deposits of tumor cells.

This set of different diagnoses as organizing root metaphors, all candidates for axioms of the system at initial presentation, is called in medicine the "differential diagnosis." By determining a better "fit" for the entire symptom complex in terms of current physiologic theory, a single diagnosis will be chosen.

The resulting inductive argument, just as with the deductive argument in Euclid's geometry, will create a coherent logical formulation. This coherent formulation will provide the causal links whereby intended human possibility is grasped and actualized.

But this inductive proof cannot claim for itself the same degree of certainty that a deductive proof provides. This is because its axiom (diagnosis) is not considered the necessarily-given condition of the patient. It is not given as true, as is the axiom of the "point" in Euclid's deductive geometry. It is only one of several possible axioms that might explain the rash - though one will be found to establish a better utilitarian fit between the patient's symptoms and current pathophysiologic theory.

Eddington described this problem of induction in this way: An inductive explanation "is introduced which, however plausible, can scarcely be considered incontrovertible. We can show that a certain structure will explain all the phenomena; we cannot show that nothing else will." [109]

Therefore, taking logical necessity as it is derived from inductive reasoning as the foundation of "truth" in a scientific formulation would seem to be problematic for science as well as for medical decision making.

From the perspective of possibility theory, this is a false problem, for the goal is to derive coherence for the sake of causality, not to "establish the truth" of the formulation. The truth of a formulation, from the perspective of possibility theory, emerges from its utility in the grasp of possibility.

The problem of inductive reason in science

Since the axioms of a deductive proof are taken to be true *a priori*, and since its theorems follow necessarily from these axioms, deduction was the presumed guarantor of truth for scientific conclusions. Euclid's deductive system of geometry represented the paradigm of this certainty.

For this reason the predominance of induction over deduction in science posed a theoretical problem. The axioms of inductive proof are empirical. Their a priori nature as truth (i.e., applicable in every instance) is not established. Therefore, in an inductive system, unlike the deductive system of Euclidean geometry, there is notjust one set of possible axioms. There are, in theory, multiple possible axioms in terms of which to explainthe derived findings.

For instance, unlike Euclid's axiom of the "point," a formulation such as the first law of thermodynamics has no proven foundation in truth except that it has been found thus far to apply in all observed situations. As Max Planck pointed out, this theory of conservation of energy is an "experimental" law, so that "its validity one day may have to be restricted." [110] This leaves the defense of certainty in scientific formulations exposed.

A simple and analogous impression in geometry exists when displaying three points at equal distances from each other on a flat plane, as shown below.

To place these three dots equally spaced, one might construe them either as the corners of an equilateral triangle or as the terminal ends of the three 120-degree arcs of a circle, as shown below.

Shall we say that these three dots "are" the corners of a triangle, or that they are the ends of equal arcs of a circle? Either explanation will do, rendering an uncertainty as to the definition of the points.

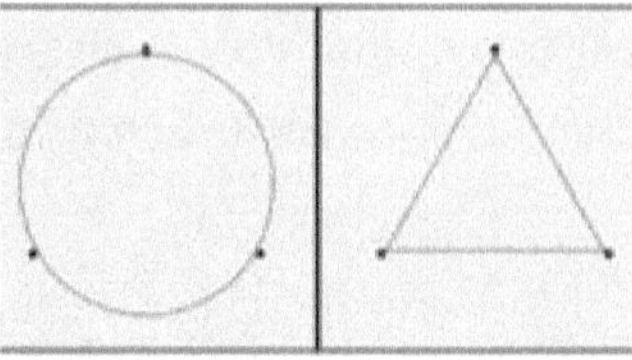

An analogous situation in medicine would be the hematologic disorder called "monoclonal gammopathy." In this disorder, the white blood cells of the body, that are responsible for producing the proteins of the immunesystem, begin to over-produce a strain of molecule. This over-production results in an impaired immune system, anemia, hyper-viscosity, and organ failure.

Historically it is not clear whether one should think of monoclonal gammopathy as a kind of cancer such as leukemia or as an immune dysregulation, such as the disorder called Waldenstrom macroglobulinemia. In some instances it can be fashioned with equal validity in terms of either of these root metaphors.

The findings and causal relations of monoclonal gammopathy will be defined based upon which root metaphor is chosen, that is, in terms either of "immune dysregulation" or of "cancer." These findings, so described, will lead back to the chosen root metaphor as their necessary conclusion. This will take the form of an evidence-based logical argument, that is a "proof," that the patient "has" either an immune disorder or cancer.

Because of this uncertainty in inductive reasoning, the Euclidean deductive system, whose axioms such as the point and line were considered to be given as true, was held out as the paradigm of logical formulation for science, not susceptible to the inherent uncertainties of inductive logic.

However, this privileged position of Euclidean geometry, and of deductive reasoning itself, was brought into question by developments in science in the 20th century.

An axiom of the Euclidean deductive system that was taken to be given as true is the parallel postulate, as shown below. It states simply that two lines that cross a third line at the same angle will never cross each other.

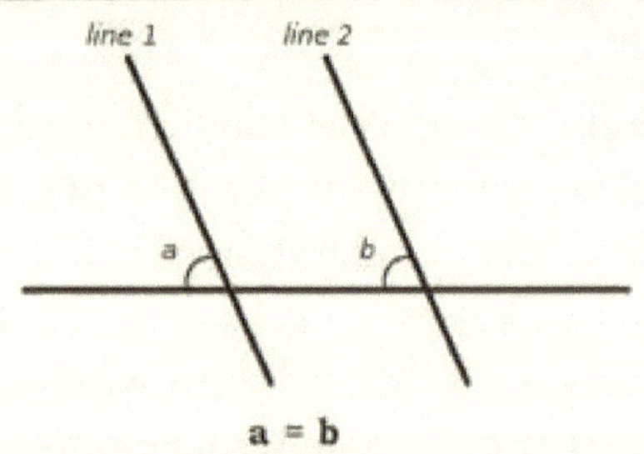

converse of) Euclid's Parallel Postulate

The truth of this postulate was famously brought into question by relativity theory. According to relativity theory, space-time is essentially curved. Therefore, all lines eventually intersect, even if the initial angles 'a' and 'b' are equal. It proved necessary to adopt alternative geometries for relativity theory, built upon axioms from which the demonstrable theorems could be derived.

This appeared to threaten the given truth of geometry based on deduction, because it demonstrated that the coherence of geometry is a creative enterprise. It relies upon an inductive process of choosing among, even creating, axioms for the sake of coherence, instead of finding them as necessarily given.

Fixing the problem of induction

The true dilemma in science is not so much how to establish truth despite induction, but to explain why the scientific mind feels compelled to accept the validity of inductive constructs in lieu of axioms first established as true in every instance. As Karl Popper asked, "Are we justified in reasoning from instances of which we have experience to other instances of which we have no experience?" [163]

For instance, why does the physicist rely upon the notion of the conservation of energy as a fundamental law of thermodynamics, though it cannot have been empirically demonstrated to be true in every possible application?

Similarly, why does the physician, knowing that all diagnostic entities will be found in time to be wanting as historical artifacts, feel secure nevertheless in proceeding forward in the care of a patient with these cognitive constructs?

Karl Popper sought to answer this question, and to vindicate the use of induction, by introducing the notions of "falsifiability" and "verisimilitude."

He pointed out that the conclusions of inductive

argument, because of their empiric nature, can be tested. Even if they are not provable as final truth, they are at least susceptible to being proven to be un-true. That is, they are falsifiable. This permits them to serve as steps in the progression to an idealized final truth, grasped mythologically by the notion of "verisimilitude." Thereby the scientist who holds to the discovery myth and believes in a discoverable truth can in good faith rely upon inductive reasoning.

In this way Popper redeemed the "discovery" myth of science. His notion of verisimilitude salvaged truth as an independently-discoverable feature of reality, toward which the researcher can aim.

Induction as a false problem

From the perspective of possibility theory, however, this redemption is both unnecessary and misleading. The sense of "truth" evoked by a formulation is the sense of its effective grasp of possibility for actualization. Its logical coherence exists only as a tool toward this end.

That is, coherence, in the form of an inductive proof, persuades the investigator not because the investigator is fooled by inductive logic, or because inductive logic is a step toward some idealized truth called verisimilitude, but because what the investigator actually perceives is the effective grasp of intended possibility.

From the perspective of possibility theory, the axiomatic "laws of nature" are valid, not because they are demonstrated ahead of time to be the only explanations of nature, but because they satisfy the need for logical coherence, even if this coherence is based on induction. For instance, the truth of Newton's first law lies in its utility in satisfying the anthropic need for"permanence of substance." It thereby applies to all knowable reality because it applies to all knowing.

Logical certainty in mathematics

By the 20th century, it had been widely assumed that,as logical proof establishes the truth of a scientific formulation, the laws of logic therefore represent the conditions of truth itself. Bertrand Russell and A. N. Whitehead set out to harness this assumption to address a problem that had come to plague modern science since the time of Newton.

The problem they sought to address arose from the centrality of mathematics to modern science. One needed somehow to establish the independent truth of mathematics to support mathematics as a foundation for science.

The occult origin and reference of number posed a barrier to this exploration. As we demonstrated, the referent of number is pure intentionality regarding possibility. However, from the natural perspective, this reference to possibility is not acknowledged, so that number appears to refer to itself only. It appears to have no external referent with which to ground it.

Without an external referent, there appears no way to prove the validity of mathematics. Without this, the foundation of mathematical science remains dubious. Russell and Whitehead set out to resolve this dilemma by demonstrating a foundation for mathematics in the laws of logic, and so in the presumed foundation of truthitself.

As logical proof appeared to secure the truth of an objective scientific formulation, the laws of logic appeared to be the foundation of truth. Thus, Russell and Whitehead set out to ground the truths of mathematics by deriving them as theorems from the laws of logic as axioms. Thereby it seemed that the truth of mathematics could be secured. This was their project called Principia Mathematica.

Just as with the axioms of Euclidean geometry, this project required taking the laws of logic as given, as true in their own right. It was on this rock that the project of Principia Mathematica foundered.

In the task of constructing a logically-coherent system, it was shown to be necessary to create axioms of logic as they were needed for the sake of deriving the desired mathematical theorems from them. Thus, the project revealed itself to be inherently ad hoc. As the mathematician Howard DeLong said, mathematics "demands an intrinsic creativity in order to progressively define the reality to which it refers." [165] This limitation of logical systems was famously codified in Godel's proof, demonstrating that a fully consistent logical system is necessarily incomplete.

The apparent synthetic nature of logical systems seemed to subvert the goal of Principia Mathematica, that was to formulate a foundation for mathematics.

From the perspective of possibility theory, however, the creative nature of axiomatic systems is to be expected. The goal of logical proof is not to establish an independent truth. It is to create the logical coherence whereby possibility is grasped. The "truth" of a formulation is established not by logical coherence, but by the deeper agenda of the grasp of possibility that is obtained through the tool of logical coherence.

Though the agenda of Principia Mathematica appeared to be subverted, this nevertheless helped to open the door to explore the mythological role of logic and of number. Number and logic are in fact related to each other, as number refers to pure intentionality as grasped by metaphor, and logic is the codified conditions of coherence in metaphor induction.

The mythological function of "truth"

As we have seen, the hypnotic nature of metaphor induction causes its products to appear discovered as the ends-in-themselves. Therefore, when one senses that an objective formulation effectively grasps intended possibility, this is construed as an attribute of the formulation itself. The formulation is said to "be true." Formulations are conceived of as "just true in their own right" as Nagel put it. [160]

The discovery myth harnesses this impression of "truth" as a characteristic of objective formulation, to facilitate the creative process of metaphor induction. By positing truth itself as a discoverable feature of reality, the scientist envisions herself as "seeking for the truth."

This guides the formulation of a metaphorical graspof possibility until the sense of grasped possibility is satisfied. One feels that one has "arrived at the truth," or that the "truth has been found."

To acknowledge the mythological role of truth is not to say that there "is no truth." Such a statement would be an abuse of the mythological function of "truth." This would be to fall prey to nihilism as it is defined by Nietzsche. According to Nietzsche, when we recognize that our truth is not the final truth, it "now seems as if there were no meaning at all in existence, as if everything were in vain." [161]

Instead, invoking Nietzsche's notion of the "revaluation of value," we can come to understand that truth, functioning as a myth, serves an end beyond itself.

The mythological function of duality

Through the evolved brain, the universe manifests itsself-awareness as individual consciousness. As Nagel said, conscious life is the process of "the universe gradually waking up and becoming aware of itself." [59] The brain has evolved to create the theater of the mind in which the universe experiences itself in twocomplementary ways: as the perceived world, and asperceiver of the world. As the Buddhist scholar Abe saidin his introduction to The Awakening of Faith, the mind exists at the intersection of two ways of seeing, that "differ epistemologically but not ontologically." [67]

To manage these separate experiences, the myth posits two separate substances: mind and matter. The notion of an explanatory gap arises from our inability to causally link these two "substances" in consciousness, asthey are experienced fundamentally differently. One is the universe as perceived, the other is the universe perceiving, both experiences created in the brain. Only the perceived world, however, is susceptible to being made into an object of analysis.

This gap persists because we fail to appreciate that these two experiences are simply one source knowing itself as apart-from itself through the agency of the brain. As Ernst Cassirer said, "The apparent dualism, the rupture in the fabric of 'existence,' is in truth nothing other than the result of a necessary duality of 'sight.' [197]

The objective world that arises in the mind for the subject is no less a part of the domain of possibility in which the subject perceives herself as a manifestation. As Eddington said, "The physical no less than the mystical significance of the scene is not there; it is here -in the mind."

This does not mean that matter does not really exist. It means that its existence, as matter, is an artifact of the reconstitution of the universe in mind for the purpose of the self-perception of the universe. As Eddington said...

The actuality of Nature is like the beauty of Nature. We can scarcely describe the beauty of a landscape as non-existent when there is no conscious being to witness it; but it is through consciousness that we can attribute a meaning to it. And so it is with the actuality of the world. If actuality means 'known to the mind' then it is a purely subjective character of the world; to make it objective we must substitute'knowable to mind.' [3]

It is because we mistake the "objective" world as fundamental that we attempt to reduce consciousness to the terms of material objects, such as neural pathways and the molecular transmitters of neurophysiology.

Consciousness is more fundamental than the material world, not because it is a different and more fundamentalsubstance, but because it exists prior to this objectifying activity of the brain. Thus, as Eddington said, we find that the world of external objects is "incommensurable with consciousness." [61]

We bring forth mythological notions to accommodate this bifurcation in mind, such as an "internal" world of perception existing apart-from an "external" world of theperceived. This duality has great mythological utility.

Though the appearance of objects as external to the domain of consciousness is contrived by the evolved brain, this does not mean that the "external" world is an illusion and that only an "internal" world exists. It means that the division between "internal" and "external" isformulated to accommodate the experience of a knowingsubject apart from known objects.

This theoretical subject-object split was codified famously in Descartes' proposition, "I think, therefore I am." With the phrase "I think," Descartes projected the metaphor "I" onto the experience of perceiving, so that itappears given. As he said, he discovered "when I recently examined the questions whether anything in the world existed, and I recognized from the very fact that I examined this question that it was very evident that I myself existed." [198] In this way he harnessed the illusion of metaphor induction, with reference to the "I," to establish a certain starting point for science.

The resulting theoretical subject-object split serves as an effective scientific myth. It frames all scientific exploration with the presumption of an objective world existing apart from the subject, and in so doing it sets up the conditions for the objective formulation as a subject- object interaction, whereby intended possibility is actualized.

The hazard of duality

The downside of this myth is that the subject is not acknowledged as a part of the world that she has as her world. The act of metaphor induction, in which the "I" is created, reifies the split between the subject and object.

The notion of "dual" substances was elaborated upon by John Locke, extending the myth in terms of an "internal versus external" aspect of reality. He distinguished between the "primary" qualities of objects external to the mind and their "secondary" qualities manifesting only in mind, what we today call "qualia."

These secondary qualities according to Lock exist only in a qualified way, for they are the effects of the primary qualities manifesting through the filters of perception, such as our impression of "color" when the wavelength of a particular photon reaches our eye. This is a notion going back as far as Democritus, associated with his notion of the atom, wherein he said that "Sweet exists by convention, bitter by convention; atoms and Void exist in reality." [202]

From the perspective of the myth of dualism it would seem not possible for the subject to know the source of scientific truth directly, that being the object external to the mind. As Schopenhauer said, what we know "is not a sun and an earth, but only an eye that sees a sun, a hand that feels an earth." [158]

But the mind, by virtue of being a manifestation of the universe, does know the source, as the direct apprehension of possibility, prior to the objectifying activity of the brain.

Naive efforts to resolve the dilemma of dualism, that do not appreciate its nature as a myth, have in general attempted to reduce one arm of the mind-matter duality to the other. That is, to say either that mind is made of matter, or that all of matter exists only in mind.

From the perspective of possibility theory, however, this option arises from an unnecessary surrender to an "internal-versus-external" myth. We have believed erroneously that we must choose between an "internal" or an "external" world, rather than recognizing this as an artificial construct, arising to accommodate the two ways in which the universe knows itself in the mind through the activity of the brain, as perceiver and as perceived.

In this naive way of seeing, the subjective features of perception are presumed to be impurities in knowledge, as only the "external" objective world is taken as true.

From the perspective of possibility theory, however, the subject is no less a manifestation of intended possibility than is the object. Therefore, the contingencies of subjective perception represent the structure of reality no less than do the features of the object. To accommodate this, the new physics incorporates the subjective features of knowing as integral to the objects of the knowable world.

Prior to the explanatory gap

In the practical world of human cognition, and in most of science, the distinction between mind and matter creates no stumbling block. This is because, in most cases, both the initial steps of a scientific investigation and its intended ends are experienced and formulated as originating and ending within the same domain, either mind or matter (usually the latter).

Therefore, no explanatory gap occurs along the theoretical causal path from beginning to end.

For example: Place your hand on the table in front of you. Take note of the firmness of the table. Though this "firmness" is in your mind, it appears to you as a feature of an object separate from you. This is not to say that there is not an object separate from you. Rather, it is to say that your experience of an object separate from you is a creation of your mind, an artifact of the evolved brain, whereby the universe comes to know itself as an object apart-from itself in the form of a knowing subject. This experience of a separate world is contrived metaphorically by you as an object apart from you. This serves the grasp of possibility for the sake of the ensuing subject-object interaction, whereby possibility, in which both you and the object partake, is actualized - for instance, whereby you move the table across the room by pushing on it.

There is no gap in such a case in the causal link

between the physical cause and the physical end. It takesplace in your mind in terms of a chain of causality that iscontrived fully in terms of physical objects, such as "I am pushing this table across the room."

Similarly, in the study of processes such as mitosis, chemical combustion, or nuclear decay, the investigator experiences both the beginning and the end of the process, the "causes" and their "effects," as observed material objects independent of the subject.

The fact that this material causal chain in fact has a metaphorical origin and functions as a myth to execute a deeper causality in the domain of possibility need not be acknowledged. It effectively can retain its appearance as the intended end in itself, from beginning to end. The beginning and the end thereby appear apart-from thesubject, with no explanatory gap emerging.

Emergence of the explanatory gap

In our brain-synthesized mode of thinking, wherein reality is presumed to begin and to end with a physical world, we try to approach the study of consciousness also in objective terms, such as a "physiology of the brain." Consciousness is said to be, for instance, "an overall effect of neuronal activities, a consequence of theincessant transformations of chemical and electrical signals in the human brain." [65] This is the beginning ofa metaphorically-construed chain of causality.

But, unlike the process of moving a table across the room, the intended end of our causal chain in this instance, awareness itself, cannot be experienced as an object apart-from the subject. It can be experienced only as awareness, as consciousness. It exists in conscious reality prior to the object-forming activity of the mind.

Therefore a "gap" is encountered in the causal chain as one approaches the intended end, that no application of a metaphor can bridge. As Eddington observed, "The primary interval relation is of an undefined nature." [66]

As an illustration: It is known that a stroke in the part of the brainstem called the "reticular activating system" (RAS) can result in impairment or loss of consciousness. The RAS therefore is conceived of metaphorically as theregulator of wakefulness. But the intended end, wakefulness itself, cannot be experienced as an object bythe researcher.

The scientist can monitor evidence of wakefulness in another person with an electroencephalogram (EEG). This subject-object interaction with the EEG will in fact have the intended effect of actualizing the directly- apprehended evidence of wakefulness in the other - much like moving a table across the room. But, unlike the EEG or table, wakefulness itself can be experienced only as awareness. Thus, an unbridgeable "gap" is created in the causal chain for the examining researcher.

That is, a special problem arises when attempting to make consciousness itself into an "object" of analysis. Consciousness cannot be experienced as an object in the mind, for it is the pre-objective source of objects. As Planck said, "We cannot get behind consciousness." [63] Or as Eddington lamented, "Such a world can perhaps begrasped, but not pictured by the brain." [54]

An attempt to reduce consciousness to an object of study creates a paradox that is experienced tacitly by the researcher. That is, to study consciousness in the mind, itwould have to be reduced to an object for the subject. But consciousness is itself the pre-objective field that is the source of objects. Thus, to reduce consciousness to an object in mind would be to subvert its pre-objective state.

For this reason, the chain of objective causality is broken as it travels from an initially contrived objective grasp, such as the brain as a physical organ, or an electroencephalogram (EEG), and attempting to arrive at the final phenomenon, the experience of consciousness.

Closing the explanatory gap in brain physiology

We are left with the dilemma of formulating an objective science of consciousness, even while knowing that consciousness, as the source of objects, cannot be experienced as, or reduced to, an object. It can be experienced only as awareness itself. This is not because we cannot "find" the object that causes consciousness (the correlates of consciousness), but that consciousness is more fundamental than what we call the object.

The challenge is to build a science of consciousness, conceived of in terms of the objects of neurophysiology, that explains consciousness as the source of the very metaphorical tools in mind that make up this very examination. In this way, that is by understanding brain physiology as a myth, the mind can create a study of itself without paradox.

For instance, some have loosely proposed that the "indeterminism" of quantum theory suggests a way to account for the apparent non-deterministic nature of free will. Even if quantum theory does not "explain" free will, it still can help to liberate the science of consciousness from the straight jacket of physical determinism, as it makes plausible a physical reduction of consciousness that is non-deterministic.

A more fulsome quantum theory of consciousness might explain how objective formulations come into being in response to direct apprehension of the universe. Thereby, this objective theory would recursively alert the investigator to its own mythological origin, and so circumvent the causal gap.

Such a quantum theory of consciousness was proposed in the 20th century by Roger Penrose and Stuart Hameroff. [68] Their theory was based on the discovery of a microtubular infrastructure of the brain. If these microtubules are of an atomic structure that can accommodate quantum-level processes, such as entanglement and coherence, then one can imagine a connection with the universe at the quantum level, and thus consciousness as a reconstituted manifestation of the universe.

Thus understood, the brain might be conceived of not as a tool for "perceiving the world," but as a tool for channeling the universe into a form of cosmic self-perceiving, constituted as the theater of the mind.

It makes a difference whether we conceive of the brain simply as an insular substrate of consciousness, versus as a channel through which the universe becomes aware of itself. Without this external referent, the content and meaning of consciousness are presumed to begin and end at the artificial physiological limits of the brain.

For instance, such a sentiment is reflected in the words of the objectivist philosopher Ayn Rand when addressing the question of the meaning of life. As she said, "This, my body and spirit, this is the end of the quest." [159] This is a positivism that tragically dispenses with perception of the cosmic domain, and of the other, as essential to the fullness of the self.

If consciousness is identical to a cluster of brain cells, then its significance comes to an end with the death of these cells. However, if these cells are a channel whereby the universe becomes aware of itself, in the form of consciousness, then consciousness has a cosmic reality and significance that extends beyond the brain, just as music exists beyond the ear, though the ear is necessary for the hearing and existence of music as music.

The myth of morality

Any objective formulation will evoke awareness of possibility at some level. In this way and to this degree itcreates the moral condition by creating responsibility forwhat is known. The moral power of a formulated preceptresides in this evocative capacity. As we saw in the last chapter, a phrase can be made into an explicitly moral proposition by adding terms such as "should" or "ought," that combine an assertion of obligation with the future tense, and thereby invoke the question of responsibility for possibility. Ethics is the discipline of inducing such response through moral precept.

Metaphor induction causes the created moral precept to appear discovered as a condition of responsibility, rather than as a means of precipitating a sense of responsibility. Therefore, the moral act appears simply to be fidelity to precepts as discovered.

Moral Precept. *Susan Saandholland on Midjourney*

To facilitate the creation of moral precepts as well-formed objects for the subject, the discovery myth begins by positing a moral reality wherein these precepts exist to be "found." This moral reality is further imbued with characteristics that evoke perception of possibility, so that these precepts, formulated as discovered, assume these characteristics in their formulation.

The notion of a preexisting domain of moral values engenders an expectation of universal consensus. That is, if moral action is fidelity to discoverable precepts that are true in themselves, then one would expect all agents eventually to come together around a common set of moral precepts.

However, the only way in which morality is a universal agenda is in the shared struggle for evocation of a sense of responsibility to possibility. It cannot hope to be the sharing of a set of logically-consistent precepts, for no finite set of precepts can capture all of possibility as it presents to consciousness. The content of moral precepts therefore must manifest differently to accommodate different communities and situations.

Universal consistency within a community has social value in its own right, of course. Thus, the trajectory of the moral argument will be toward consistency, as a community strives for a shared sense of responsibility. The formulation also will evolve as a logical argument. But this logical argument will accomplish its moral end through evocation of a sense of responsibility, not by the persuasion of logical necessity in itself.

Utilitarianism as myth

The moral myth of "utilitarianism" emerges from the observation that moral precepts tend to facilitate what are called "good outcomes." According to utilitarianism, therefore, it is the "greater good" in itself, existing ahead of time, that determines the moral end.

Positing the existence of a "greater good" ahead

of time serves to promote the metaphorical grasp of possibility in these terms. However, the formulation of the useful moral precept is driven by apprehension of possibility, using the mythological terms of the "greater good," not existing ahead of time, but as if discovered.

For example, imagine a tragic situation in which the driver of a car is forced to choose between collision witha child who is standing on one side of a road, versus fouradults standing on the other side of the road, as the car must swerve in one direction or the other.

Neither option, the life of the child nor of the four adults, is the obvious "greater good" on first encounter. The logical argument that one or the other is the greater good will serve to evoke a search for a sense of responsibility to possibility.

One might argue that, as life itself is the greater good, the greater good in this situation is served by saving more people. Thus, one should swerve away from the four adults, and into the path of the child. But that choicemight offend the sensitivity of an adult, who might argue that the greater good is represented by the sacrifice of an adult to spare the innocence of a child, and that one is being "less than a human" by not being willing to die for this end - thereby turning the logical argument on its head, in the service of a deeper sense of what it means tobe human.

What this shows is that the logical argument of the "greater good" is, in itself, not sufficient to establish the moral precept. The logical argument serves as an edifice upon which to precipitate a sense of possibility.

We see that moralizing is an inherently incomplete

process, because the domain of possibility is infinite, and the objective formulation elicits perception of possibilityonly to a bounded, perspectival degree at any one time.

One might argue that a moral actor is wrong in his moral decision because he is mistaken in his assessment of the "degree of possibility" served by his moral act. However, the morality of an act is not determined or constituted by the degree of possibility that it grasps, but by the sense of responsibility that awareness of possibility evokes. It is the reality of this sense, not the degree of possibility, that creates the moral condition. The moral actor has no choice but to respond to, or to turn away from, his impression. This is the existential condition of the moral situation.

Similarly, the argument that morality is based on thea priori greater good of a particular ideology is the crucible upon which Marxism, as an ethical system, failed in the 20th century. As the Marxist theoristAnthony Giddens pointed out, the presumed superiority of materialist theory in the 20th century created a "wishto establish a natural science of society, which wouldpossess the same sort of logical structure and pursue thesame achievements as the sciences of nature." [168] Bytaking this physical reality as logical proof of the greatergood, Marxism argued that any and all means were justified in pursuing the final end of historicalmaterialism. As Trotsky said, "lying, frame-up, betrayal,murder, and so on" are "permissible and obligatory" forthe sake of the historical mission of the proletariat. [169]However, as was laid bare by the ensuing Stalin purges, the gulag archipelago, and the campaign of Pol Pot, the counterweight in consciousness of perceived possibility established itself as the moral end, regardless of the logical persuasion of the materialistic ideology. If the "means" to an end offend conscience, then consciousness will require that these means be reformulated as the new ends.

Since the power of a moral formulation lies in its evocative capacity relative to perception of possibility, it is reasonable to ask why one does not simply formulate the desired moral end in terms of "greater possibility." The reason this does not work is that the notion of possibility itself is not an effective myth. The term "possibility" does not itself effectively evoke perception of possibility.

The term "possibility" serves as a myth only to grasp the universe as it comes to us in the form of anticipation of actualization. It does not otherwise help in its grasp. That is, as a metaphor, "possibility" fails to evoke the interactive grasp of itself, for it does not capture the features of itself that are known only in direct apprehension. For this, more fulsome metaphors are needed.

For example, the early 20th century movement called "social Darwinism" was based on an argument of greater human possibility as end in itself. Using the eugenics laws in America, nearly fifty thousand women who were deemed feeble-minded were forcibly sterilized, with the intention of removing an "inferior" strain from the gene pool.

This practice came to an end when Nazis Germany took up the project of eugenics with more programmatic ardor. It seems there was something more offensive in cruelty than in feeblemindedness, something less desirable existentially for the evolution of humansociety, despite the logic of eugenics. Terms such as "compassion" emerged to grasp this deeper sense of possibility in objective form so that it might be intended as the greater end.

Terms that evoke possibility

Though any metaphor that evokes perception of possibility can serve a moral function, there are certain metaphors that recur in moral thought because they centrally touch upon perception of possibility. Two such metaphors are "life" and the "other."

The process of possibility self-actualizing, such as the growth of a plant bending toward the sun, or the mitotic dividing of cells, or the migrating of birds in the seasons, is what is called "life" - not by convention, but by recognition. This is why Schweitzer's formulation of the "reverence for life," or the Jain concept of ahimsa, serve as fundamental moral precepts. Each, serving as anend in itself, addresses reverence for the perception of possibility that it evokes.

Similarly, the "golden rule," stated as "do unto others as you would have them do unto you," is always of moral consequence. This is because what we call the"other" is nothing but awareness of possibility manifesting as consciousness. A star in the heavens, or arock on the seashore, though they evoke awe, are notrecognized as possessing consciousness, and so do notbecome an object of moral approbation in the same way. An illustration of the positing of a moral reality, for the purpose of formulating moral precepts in terms of their discovery therein, is Kant's moral proposition that acting with regard to the other is necessarily of moral consequence because of the logical nature of the other. Thereby his myth posits into the moral universe two features that engage the moral sense - logical coherence and the "other."

To accommodate the observed utility of the logical structure of the moral precept, Kant posited the imperative that one should, "act only in that maxim through which you can at the same time will that it should become a universal law," that is, in such a way that it is logically persuasive under any circumstance, that is to say of its own nature.

Then, to explain and accommodate the fact that the "other" always is an object of moral approbation, Kant conflated the notions of logical structure and the other with the proposition that "a rational being belongs to the kingdom of ends as a member, when, although he makes its universal laws, he is also himself subject to these laws." That is, Kant argues that the other is necessarily an object of moral approbation because of his logical nature.

Good faith versus bad faith

The formulation of a moral precept with the intent to respond to possibility is moral argument made in "good faith." Conversely, the formulation of a moral argument with the intent to obfuscate or to deflect perception of possibility in the name of objectivity is moral argument made in "bad faith." This distinction is difficult to see overtly, as each appears as devotion to objectivity.

In the last chapter we took as our example the definition of elective abortion as "killing a life." If this definition is construed to save the life of an unborn child, it is an instance of good faith. However, if the same argument is intended to obfuscate awareness of harm done to a vulnerable pregnant woman, then it is an instance of bad faith. In each case the same outcome is proposed, but with different intention.

This dichotomy manifests also on a social scale, described by Sartre in his Critique of Dialectical Reason. All social groups, such as religious, political, governmental, familial, or professional societies such as medicine, emerge initially in response to a communally shared perception of possibility. The objective creeds of the group emerge to grasp and actualize this shared end.

In time (inevitably, according to Sartre) the devotion to these creeds devolves into devotion to mere survival of the group. The creeds no longer serve their initial mythological role. One now takes advantage of their appearance as ends in themselves to render a test of purity, sometimes posing a mortal threat to dissenters.

In this, the function of the creeds devolves from affirmation of possibility in good faith to a tool of oppression in bad faith, though the overt devotion to the creed does not change. Thereby the group loses its authenticity and begins to decay as a human group, as it no longer exists to affirm the domain of possibility that defines the human condition.

Medicine risks this path by mistaking science, in the form of molecular biology or information technology, or worse, commercial enterprise, as end in itself, rather than as a means of actualizing human possibility apprehended directly in the doctor-patient relationship.

The decision to use evidence-based formulations in good-faith requires the courage to address open-ended possibility as it is apprehended directly in the doctor- patient relationship, and as the social agenda of medicine. In this way, all decisions are "rooted in the courage of being," as Tillich describes them, giving cosmic meaning to the therapeutic decision. [195]

The mythological notion of time

The mind creates the notion of "time" as a reference to possibility with regard to its states of actualization. In this way, time is a means of referring to the entire domain of possibility. One refers to the domain of possibility in its entirety as the "fullness of time." Just as with the perception of possibility, time, as a perception of actuality, is tangible, and is felt as non-reversible, and in this sense as directional.

The "past" and the "future" refer to our sense of various features of the domain of possibility itself. What we call the "future" is our sense of the open-ended nature of possibility. As Tillich said, the future "is genuine only if it is open." [174] We perceive the future as real because we are aware of it as a feature of possibility.

Similarly, the "past" is the nature of possibility as it manifests as actuality. The past does not lose its fundamental connection to open-ended possibility with this manifestation. As Tillich pointed out, the past "becomes something different through everything new that happens." [175]

Debate over a specific "historical fact" is essentially an argument about the nature of possibility itself, as it manifests in actuality. This is why questions of historiography animate us, and why historiography always is an act of interpretation. Our sense of the natureof possibility informs our reconstruction of what we call the "past." This reconstruction is perspectival. In composing history as a reified past, we risk mistaking our metaphorical reconstruction as given. We run the risk of disconnecting the past from its ground in possibility.

For instance, in his seminal work, The Quest of the Historical Jesus, the theologian-physician Albert Schweitzer explained that an attempt to defend a transcendental truth in terms of the actuality of past events is problematic since the description is perspectival and therein isolates it from the infinite domain of possibility in which its truth lies. Regarding the real Jesus, for example, "How much we possess of him depends on how much we let him tell us of the kingdom of God." [117] - that is, how much of the domain of possibility is made apparent through the notion of him.

As an artifact of metaphor induction, time appears given as an end in itself, thus with no external reference to a deeper transcendental realm of possibility. For this reason, the measurement of time, in any form of provisional "clock," appears circular: Measured time appears definable only in terms of its chosen clock.

Time is indeed measured by us by indexing it to a common unit of change, such as the rotation of the Earth, or the vibrations of an atom of cesium. But this selected index is chosen because it is a common measureof the actualization of possibility. Therefore, it is the actualization of possibility that is the true referent of time.

This reference to possibility gives to time both a subjective and an objective nature. They are different in use, but related to each other in reality. The subjective experience of "time slowing down" or of "time standing still" is a sense of "nothing happening" in the deepestsense of the actualization of possibility.

Provisional Clock. *Susan Saandholland on Midjourney*

The objective measurement of time with a clock, on the other hand, is simply evoking this same experience, but referencing it to a shared measure of actualization.

We see the reference to the domain of possibility when we recognize the utilitarian nature of time. As Sartre said, the past, present and future "must not be envisaged as a collection of 'data' to be added together... but as the structured moments of an original synthesis." [118] Or, as the celebrated 20th-century Romanian orchestra maestro Celibidache said, regarding the element of tempo in music: "What is tempo?... There is no reality behind it. Time is a condition by which the multitude of information contained in sound can be reduced to a unity." [171]

To accommodate the domain of possibility beyond

actuality, the new physics adds the dimension of time to the three geometric dimensions of space. It is difficult for the non-physicist to imagine the resulting four- dimensional "space-time," because it is difficult to visualize a four-dimensional grid by which it is measured. As Capra pointed out, this is easier for the physicist because of the abstract mathematical formalismof theory. [21]

However, this does not mean that a geometric grid is the better model with which to visualize possibility. Unlike a grid, the non-physicist (and likely the physicist)experiences the domain of possibility directly. It is easierto "visualize" this domain if we use a more intuitive model that is consistent with how the domain of possibility is experienced. For instance, one might imagine possibility as a flowing stream.

We refer to all of possibility, regardless of actuality, in transcendental terms such as "eternity." As Spinoza said, "In Eternity there is no such thing as when, before, or after." [203] This is consistent with the "block" modelof the universe, as described by Eddington: "In a perfectly determinate scheme the past and future may be regarded as lying mapped out... Events do not happen; they are just there." [112] We do not experience time in the "present." We experience eternity. We refer to our participation in this eternity however in terms of time, that is, in terms of actualization.

Mortality and the myth of time

Understanding time as a myth gives to us a window to understanding the anxiety associated with mortality inthe clinical setting.

Time and Eternity. *Susan Saandholland on Midjourney*

Tillich introduced the notion of the "eternal now" to underscore the fact that what we call the "present" is our experience of participation in eternity. This is at odds with the notion of time as a fleeting end in itself, with no reference to a deeper domain. The mythological notion of time would seem to require an endless extension of the present into the future for our participation in eternity. But Tillich warned against this notion, arguing that eternity "is neither timelessness nor the endlessness of time." [114]

Our encounter with death is associated with a peculiar form of anxiety precipitated by our awareness of eternity. This was expressed by the second-century astronomer, Ptolemy, in this way: "I know that I am mortal by nature, and ephemeral; but when I trace at my pleasure the windings to and fro of the heavenly bodies I no longer touch the earth with my feet: I stand in the presence of Zeus himself..." [176] Indeed, when we stareat the nighttime stars we tangibly see the eternity in which we partake.

The dilemma of mortality might be stated this way: ifconsciousness is not merely awareness of the universe through the evolved brain, if it is the cosmos manifesting as self-awareness in the form of consciousness through the evolved brain, then does not consciousness have an eternal significance, an immortality of sorts on its own?

This question helps us to understand why the peculiar concern over death, manifesting as the pain of grief,cannot be accounted for merely by the loss of something precious, such as the loss of one's favorite slippers, or even as the loss of a dear friend. The distinction is not simply a difference of degree. There is a discrepancy of sorts that takes the form of an intolerable warping of the universe, an appearance that is ontologically perplexing.

As the novelist Julian Barnes wrote of the death of his wife, it is "unimaginable: not just its length and depth, but its tone and texture, its deceptions and false dawns, its recidivisms." [177]

That which was perceived to be eternal appears to have passed away with death. The eternity that one knewthrough the eyes of the beloved, the eternity that was the reason for the peculiar kind of love that we have for the other, appears to cease to be when their brain dies.

To accommodate this perplexing apposition of the sense of eternity with the awareness of death, the mind attempts cognitive reconciliation, such as turning to the notion of an afterlife. The philosopher Hegel proposed inhis notion of "bad infinity," that we create the notion of an "after-life" because we fail to appreciate the eternity in this life. Since our terms for life in this world do not accommodate a sense of participation in a transcendent domain, we create an "other-worldly" notion for this. Wefind ourselves "awaiting death" for participation in eternity.

But consciousness in the present partakes in eternity. The brain, as that organ through which the universe manifests as individual consciousness, does in fact pass away. But the brain is not the insular substrate of consciousness. The substrate of consciousness is the eternal universe as it manifests by means of the constituting activity of the brain. The longing after an afterlife is simply the desire to affirm the validity of the sense of the eternal in this life.

The peculiar suffering of grief occurs because we mistake the finite brain as the source of the infinite content of consciousness. This is not to minimize the suffering at loss of a beloved other. For in the beloved the eternity that one loves is made manifest.

Indeed, this is why it is therapeutic for the grieving person to be asked to recollect features of the beloved. This act of "recollection" is in fact a form of perception. It affirms the reality of those features of the deceased that are loved, and acknowledges their persistence in the domain of eternity. Thus, Einstein could say, when eulogizing the loss of a close friend, "For those of us who believe in physics, the distinction between past, present and future is only a stubbornly persistent illusion."

As the 13th-century Sufi poet Rumi said, death is "our wedding with eternity." [179] It is the moment we are singularly forced to acknowledge the eternal aspect of ourselves or our beloved that had been made intelligible to us through temporal existence.

Mortality ironically encourages this modulation in thought. As Rilke said, "death does not wound us without, at the same time, lifting us toward a more perfect understanding of this being and of ourselves." [180]

Or as Tillich says, "...there is death, that as the limit of the finite inevitably poses the question of the meaning of finitude, thus leading beyond finitude." [181] Therefore, grief is not a "resignation" to loss, but a struggle for "reconciliation" between our sense of eternity and the appearance of loss. Sigmund Freud noted that "in the unconscious every one of us is convinced of his immortality." [178] It might be more accurate to say that in the unconscious every one of us knows of his or her immortality, and that grief is a struggle to reconcile this with the appearance of death.

Death as an illusion

This requires a revision of our way of thinking about death. If consciousness is an expression of the infinite universe, that is, its self-knowing through the agency of the brain, then death as finality is in some manner an illusion.

What we call the "soul" is our awareness of, and thus our need to put a name to, this tangible instantiation of the eternal order. When we further perceive the soul to have an eternal nature, it is because we sense the eternal order of which it is an instantiation. Herein we recognizewhat is ultimately real about the soul.

This does not mean that the individual soul survives brain death, only that the eternal order of which it is an instantiation survives. That is, the soul can be recognizedas a manifestation of an eternal order, without itself persisting in time. It can be true both that the soul has significance as a manifestation of eternity, and that this instantiation comes to an end at brain death.

The positing of an "afterlife" is driven by the need to grasp the sense of the soul as an emergent entity, as a manifestation of eternity, but combined with the mistaken notion that this requires persistence of its instantiation. As Spinoza said, men "confuse eternity with duration."

Death as Illusion. *Susan Saandholland on Midjourney*

The cessation of the soul at brain death does not invalidate its manifestation of eternity in the present. The metaphorical notion of an "afterlife" serves more to safeguard the sense of participation in eternity than to safeguard the notion of persistence, that in itself has no psychic utility.

For instance, a patient who suffers brain injury and then regains full cognitive function thereafter through rehab, but who does not recover awareness of her previous life, has not lost the eternal significance either of her previous life nor of her current consciousness state, as both are manifestations of the eternal order in the present.

As consciousness is participation in eternity, how onelives in this one precious life necessarily determines how one will live "for eternity." This determination comes to an end with the cessation of the soul at brain death. The premature cessation of Bach's Art of the Fugue at death enshrined and preserved in music a life lived in eternity.

This awareness gives meaning to the mythological notion of a "place" in eternity, such as heaven.

The physician will encounter these psychic questions and struggles routinely in practice. This concern might manifest at the time of planning for end-of-life care, asin a case of end-stage disease such as cancer or kidney failure. Or it might be voiced in more acute discussions between doctor and family regarding a dying patient.

Sometimes the lived paradox of eternity appearing to come to an end surfaces in a more cloaked way, for instance as a desperate plea for "more to be done" by way of treatment, even when all available treatment options have been exhausted. It is important to understand in this case that the patient is not simply being unreasonable; he is calling out to the physician for acknowledgment of the inconceivable nature of the situation.

The patient himself might not recognize the existential nature of the conflict. He might not be able to put into words the confounding impression of somethingeternal passing away. He might grasp for the only terms that seem appropriate for discussion with a doctor, the terms of physical treatment. In such a case, the physician must recognize that it is the apparent impermanence of existence that concerns the patient.

In the attempt at reconciliation, what consciousness eventually settles on is that, though a channel through which eternity manifested has passed away, the eternity that gave it intelligible form, and that makes it precious to us, has not. "Having eternal life" does not require an endless continuation of the present. The present is by its nature participation in the eternal order.

In the popular formulation by Kubler-Ross, grief is said to be characterized by an initial "denial." If this denial is taken to be simply resistance to a truth of loss, then the role of the physician must be to support the patient in her struggle for resignation.

However, if this "denial" is instead a refusal to acceptthe appearance of loss, because of a deeper sense of participation in eternity, then physician support means holding out for a better understanding, whether this comes in the form of the notion of an "afterlife" or otherwise grasping the eternal in this life.

Of course, the role of the physician cannot be to answer the question of mortality for the patient. Only thepatient is in a privileged position to explore this for himself. The role of the physician is simply to recognize the reality of the existential dilemma. She might simply say, "I understand." Therein she supports the patient's exploration of a reconciliation of his own making. Often this mere permission is sufficient to the patient's need.

The mythological function of the "divine"

The young medical student often is aware that his new tasks and responsibilities pose questions that are not addressed by his scientific medical education, but that pertain to his emerging social, moral and even cosmic responsibilities in the care of others. Therefore, he might seek a more encompassing philosophical context in terms of which to understand the road ahead.

Sometimes this takes the form of religious devotion and faith. At these times the notion of "God" or some other instantiation of the "divine" can become a helpful myth for the orientation of human activity. As Marcus Aurelius said in his Meditations, "you will not do any act well which concerns man without referring it to the divine." [183]

This need of the medical student is an instance of a larger human need that results in emergence of the myth of the divine, and that we will discuss below in term of possibility theory and metaphor induction.

However, it is necessary first to make an editorial note regarding the notion of the divine.

Tillich pointed out that it is difficult to discuss the notion of God in our time because it has become tangled with deceptive, even coercive, forms of thought that often emerge in a destructive way. This is an artifact of the mythological power of the notion of the divine.

To avert this distraction, we will emphasize that this book does not address the question, "Does God exist?" In light of our mythological analysis, this is a meaningless question. Rather, I wish to explore the question, "What does 'God' mean?"

I take it as given that the notion of the divine, in one form or another, has drawn human interest for all of recorded human history, and that it likely addresses some perineal need of human consciousness, even if, as Marx and Daniel Dennett have proposed, mankind would be better off rendering up this need.

The question of the nature of this need is altogether of a different kind from whether or not God exists or whether the notion of God is "true." These are not unimportant questions; but they are secondary to our main purpose. However, I reject the proposition that the notion of God "does not mean anything." This seems to me to represent an unfortunate deficit of curiosity, even sometimes an opportunistic sophistry that feeds on the low hanging fruit of popular resentment.

Tillich's proposition that human self-affirmation is "participation in the universal or divine act of self-affirmation," [184] is the same impression expressed by Descartes, in terms of the monotheistic myth of his day, that "my own existence depends entirely upon him every moment of my life." [199] I do not think that Descartes was just being pious, but that he was trying to put into words a deeper sense that he had of the origin of his own consciousness, and that Schleiermacher struggled to define as a fundamental characteristic of consciousness.

This is the same sense that receives tacit recognition in notions such as the Atman arising from Brahman in the Upanishads. To say that these are fantasy is to deny the reality of the human sensation that gives rise to them. As Max Planck said in his Scientific Autobiography, the notion of God is "the crown of the edifice of everygeneralized world view." [182]

The need for the myth of the divine

As we discussed in the last chapter, the need of the metaphor of the "divine" arises from that feature of the evolved brain wherein the universe comes to know itself as a perceiver apart from an objective world. Through this bifurcation, objective knowledge comes into being, but at the expense of alienating the knowing subject from the ground of being that she shares with the object.

From this there emerges the need of the subject to reconcile with this ground, to understand her role as manifestation of it. In common language, this emerges as the simple question "why am I here?" This interrogation results in the most consequential form of metaphor induction, which we now will explore.

In this instance, a metaphor is applied to grasp the whole of perceived possibility in a form with which the subject can interact, for the sake of this reconciliation. This results in metaphors of an all-embracing sort, such as the "God" of the monotheistic religions, or the Hindu all-embracing "Brahman," or the Buddhist "Dharma," or the Chinese principle of the "Tao," or the naturalistic god of Spinoza to which Einstein was drawn, or the "Universe" of modern science.

As the subject is a manifestation of the universe, the subject's need of God is simply the need of the universe to know individual consciousness as a manifestation of itself. As the Jewish theologian Martin Buber said, "God needs you - for that which is the meaning of your life."[123]

The creation of God, as an object in mind apart

from the subject, precipitates the subject-object interaction whereby this reconciliation can occur.

How the myth of the divine develops

The various all-encompassing root metaphors mentioned above are profound in their difference from each other. But they share a common trajectory of intention, by referring to all that can be perceived, and ina form with which the subject can interact. Their variations beyond this common feature range from the anthropic "material" Universe of science, to the "personal" God of Judaism, the "ineffable" Brahman of Hinduism, to the static "principle" of the Tao.

As in all cases of metaphor induction, the theoretical shape of the intended object, its "theology" as it were, evolves through the encounter with possibility that it provokes, taking shape in response to a pushback from possibility within the bounds of the categories of the chosen metaphor. This illuminates the nature of possibility for the subject, and thereby the role of the subject as manifestation of it.

Just as in the physical sciences, the theoretical nature of possibility takes shape in terms of the categories of the chosen metaphor. So, the subject might find herself responding to the domain of possibility, taking the form of a state of reverence, prayer, contemplation, scientific exploration, meditation, or even the self-annihilation of anatta.

For instance, from the mystical book, A Course InMiracles, the creative scope of the subject relative to possibility is described in terms of a relationship to God, saying that "in creation you are not in a reciprocal relationship to God, since He created you but you did not create Him." [185] In this way the limitation of the creative activity of the subject relative to the domain of possibility is grasped in terms of a "relationship to God."

The nature of possibility unfolds to the subject in terms of the categories of the chosen metaphor.

For instance, the open-ended nature of possibility, and the responsibility of the subject in light of this aspect of possibility, are captured in the words of the 20th-century protestant theologian, Dietrich Bonhoeffer, when he states that faith is "living unreservedly in life's duties, problems, successes and failures, experiences and perplexities," [186] and that, "Knowing the will of God is not a system of rules established from the outset. It is something new and different in each different situation in life." [167] In this way, the subject is reconciled to its ground in open-ended possibility.

How reconciliation emerges

Similarly, a central teaching of Buddhism is that suffering in its deepest sense, called "dukkha" in the Sanskrit, results from the illusion that the self exists apart from the world that it perceives. Meditation is a method conceived to deconstruct this isolated sense of a self, to permit awareness of participation in a primal unity, and so a release from suffering.

Hinduism and Buddhism reconcile the self to the universe in distinct ways. The self either is a manifestation of the whole or an illusion in apposition to the whole. In either case, the self recognizes its ultimate meaning in its relation to the whole.

Primal Unity. *Susan Saandholland on Midjourney*

In the Judeo - Christian - Muslim tradition, interaction with the domain of possibility manifests as an attempt to communicate with God in the posture of prayer. For instance, the prayer of petition is a request made of God, just as one might make a request of a parent. This act engages possibility in terms of the needs of the subject relative to the capacity of the universe. In this case, reconciliation with the whole is formulated in terms of anticipation of a response.

If one does not approach the prayer of petition as an act of reconciliation, then one mistakenly can anticipate an in-kind response - that is, a response specifically to the petitioned content of the question, rather than as an act of psychic reconciliation.

This expectation can result in existential frustration, such that expectations might have been better managed by a request to "know" or to "accept" the will of God. Thereby the meditative act of prayer would open the mind more authentically to the ground of possibility.

This formulation is similar to the Stoic notion of one's duty to open-ended possibility as that which defines the human condition. As Marcus Aurelius said ofpetitioning the gods, one must console oneself in two things: "one, that nothing will befall me which is not in accordance with the nature of the Whole; the other, thatit is in my power to do nothing contrary to my God and inward Spirit." [192] Thus the maintenance of the self means deference to the domain of possibility as thatwhich defines the subject.

As the subject is a manifestation of the domain of possibility, the nature of this domain is revealed in part simply by "looking within" at one's own nature. As Eddington said...

We see in Nature what we look for or are equipped to look for... in this sense, perhaps, the God within creates the God in Nature. But no complete viewcan be obtained so long as we separate our consciousness from the world of which it is a part. [125]

That is, God is truly created as an object in our image. However, this is not an indictment of the notionof God, for our image is necessarily God's image. As the father of Christian theology, Paul of Tarsus, said, mankind is "without excuse" because he cannot but know the nature of God.

The role of suffering in reconciliation

This helps to shed light on the role of suffering in the doctor-patient relationship. For example, the significance of Job's suffering in Jewish mythology was that he suffered to a degree that would render life not worth living if, in fact, the self is merely an end in itself. Job's dialogue "with God" regarding suffering was an exploration of the meaning of his life with regard to this question.

Job was met with an answer, from within his own psyche, formulated as a response from God. God, in the imagination of Job, expressed an essential disinterest in man's suffering relative to the majesty of the divine. Therein Job recognized his own ultimate concern relative to this infinite domain of possibility.

As Marcus Aurelius expressed, "not even for a man, as a man, is pain contrary to Nature, while he is doingthe service of a man, and if pain for him is not contraryto Nature, neither is it an evil for him." [72] Similarly, Viktor Frankl spoke of suffering as a crucible for moral growth, saying that the way in which a person accepts suffering "gives him ample opportunity to add a deeper meaning to his life." [71] Or as the 20th-century prophet Martin Luther King said, the purpose of life is not to be happy, nor to avoid pain, "but to do the will of God, come what may." [193]

In this way, the mythical interaction with God that is prompted by suffering gives the subject a sense of his meaning as part of the world that he has as his world. As John Donne petitioned of God, "Batter my heart... for I, except you enthrall me, never shall be free."

In distinction to these monotheistic myths, Buddhism addresses the question of human suffering from the perspective of possibility itself, rather than from the perspective of the subject. That is, it asks not why humanity suffers but why the Universe manifests itself as human suffering. This perspective is more consistent with the notion of the brain as the organ through which the universe knows itself as individual consciousness.

Just as in the case of the suffering of Job, the goal of the Buddhist response is not so much to answer the question of suffering, but to answer the question of the role of the subject in relation to the whole. As the Buddhist scholar Suzuki said, the mystery of suffering "can only be solved in a practical way when we attain the highest spiritual enlightenment of Buddhahood... as the water in a vessel poured into the waters of the boundless ocean, it at once perceives and realizes its nature, its destiny, and its significance in life." [194]

The role of the physician in suffering

The role of the physician is as a partner to the patient in the address of suffering, not as an end in itself, but in the context of this more fundamental meaning of life. The physician should strive to ameliorate suffering as an impediment to life lived responsibly as an agent of possibility. The physician thereby is one who goes alongwith the patient in the project of life.

The more common instance of this is the care of the patient who suffers pain. The manner in which pain is relieved can leave a patient either dependent upon drugs that dull her approach to life, or it can free her to pursuea more meaningful life. The relief of pain, while pursuedaggressively, must serve this end beyond itself.

This is on display, for example, in the peculiar therapeutic posture that the physician must assume with a patient who suffers from what is called "borderline personality disorder." This psychiatric disorder is felt to arise from an injury of abandonment at a formative age. Its characteristic lifelong pattern of fear of loneliness, resentment, anger and paranoia, makes therapeuticengagement challenging.

Yet our affection is drawn to this disorder, for it poses a question similar to Job's. On the one hand, the posture of resentment at the universe speaks a truth to us. The human condition indeed appears to be one of cosmic abandonment. The needs of the self are not a central concern of the universe. There is no force to protect the subject from deprivation. The borderline personality has been wounded by this, and lashes out against this source of her own identity.

This struggle is a self-defeating battle. Retribution against the universe will not do, for the patient is not separate from it. Rather, one finds healing in recognizingthat an unmet potential for love is known only because one is a manifestation of love. The only possible healing is a "reconciliation" with this origin - to become the lovethat one hoped for. Anger must give way to forgiveness, attack replaced with deference to the other.

The physician can model and provide safe haven for this posture by forgiving the attack if it is transferred onto the doctor. Thereby it becomes easier for the patient to become reconciled to herself.

Reconciliation

The monotheistic religions approach exploration of the subject relative to possibility in terms of humanity's "relationship" with God. This is on display in the various myths of the Torah, wherein the notion of God itself takes shape (as described by Buber in this anthropologic archeology, The Prophetic Faith). Therein this religious literature is said to be not so much "about God" but to be "what God is about."

For example, the story of Abraham and Isaac in the Torah addresses the tension between good faith and bad faith as it pertains to the perception of possibility and to objectivity.

As displayed in the story of Abraham and Isaac, the mind intuits in objectivity a moral hazard. The vested interest in objectivity can distract the subject from primary responsibility to the domain of possibility. In the story of Abraham and Isaac the mind of Abraham spawned a test to ward off this existential threat.

As the story goes, Abraham perceived in his son the prospect of a great lineage, itself derived from his primary devotion to God. This created the conditions for a good-faith devotion to possibility as it was represented by his son.

But therein existed also the conditions for bad-faith vested interest in this lineage, paradoxically threatening the source of the greatness itself.

Abraham heard the source, that is his perception of possibility imagined as God, direct him to sacrifice the object in the name of the source itself that had birthed the object. This took the macabre form of a challenge to murder his son. Thus Abraham took up a knife to kill hisson. His willingness to obey God thereby having been demonstrated, his devotion to possibility in good faith having been established, the psychic challenge fell away. He perceived the angel of God to direct him to withhold his hand from this murderous act.

Ridicule appropriately has been cast on this ancient story because of the ironic image of a compassionate God directing a father to kill his son. But this obscures its deeper mythological origin and function.

God as possibility

As the metaphor of God erupts to grasp the domain of possibility, interaction with the myth of God resides entirely at the level of possibility. As Tillich said, "everything divine transcends the split between potentiality and actuality." [189]

This places the myth of the divine in conflict with thehypnotic feature of metaphor induction, that posits the object, God in this case, as existing as a discoverable actuality in the world. This expectation, manifesting as a sense of cosmic "providence," creates an existential frustration and resentment.

For instance, when the "love" that is known to be in

the nature of possibility, as we find it within ourselves, is not found in the actual world, it is assumed that the God in terms of which it is grasped "does not exist." This is the "theodicy" of Leibniz.

As this pertains to faith, for example, this is the historic significance of the Jewish holocaust. In that instance, that which could not happen if a loving God actually exists in the world, did happen.

In his autobiographical account of events in a Nazi concentration camp, Elie Wiesel related the scene of a child being hanged to death in front of other inmate prisoners. He relates that a prisoner standing near to him said, "For God's sake, where is God?" Wiesel relates that he heard a voice within him to respond, "This is where - hanging here from this gallows." [190]

This has been taken to mean that the "god of history died at Auschwitz." What certainly died at Auschwitz was the expectation of God as actuality in the world.

A more generous interpretation, from the perspective of possibility theory, is that our outrage at this cruelty is God's outrage. Our revulsion is God's revulsion. For our consciousness is the manifestation of that domain of infinite possibility that we mythologically grasp as God.

Religious faith, if authentic, must be said to arise from a more fundamental aspect of reality than mere actuality. To be authentic, it must arise in response to perception of possibility as the foundation of actuality. Therein lies its peculiar nature and power. Through faith the believer acknowledges the reality of possibility, regardless of actuality. This gives courage to action. It is the substance of things hoped for, the evidence of things not seen, or, as Kierkegaard said, "... when in the dark night of suffering sagacity cannot see a handbreadth ahead of it, then faith can see God, since faith sees best in the dark."

The "truth" of the myth of the divine resides in the domain of possibility, even when actuality does not rise to its standard. Thus, faith requires existential courage. The courage of the physician to affirm possibility as it manifests in the patient is an instance of this faith.

Knowing God

At this point one will recognize a problem with the distinction between the experience of "having" religious faith and the "analysis" of religious faith.

The notion of the divine is experienced differently bythe faithful from how it is experienced by those who takethe divine as an object of analysis. As the historian of religion, Etienne Gilson, said, "It is psychologically interesting to know that it does one good to believe thereis a God; but that is not at all what the believer believes; what he actually believes is that there is a God." [187]

The implication is that the analysis of God as myth does not provoke reconciliation with possibility as does the experience of God as myth. However, just as the physicist who appreciates the limits of physical theory can engage with possibility by means of the notion of the"atom," so can the analyst engage with the ineffable wholeness of possibility by means of the notion of God, even while knowing it to be a metaphor.

This is made possible simply by understanding that, with human knowledge, there is no non-metaphorical vantage point. The grasp of possibility is mediated by the brain through metaphor, appearing as given. One cananalyze a metaphor, as such, even while submitting to its function as metaphor. This is why, in the relationship between faith and reason in the Middle Ages, as in the philosophies of Augustin, Al-Ghazali, and Anselm, and no less in the science in our time, faith "comes before" reason or understanding.

Every act of understanding presumes a metaphorical grasp of possibility as object of faith. One must accept metaphor as an interface to benefit from this grasp of possibility, whether this pertains to the waves of electromagnetic theory or to traditions of revelation.

The notion of the divine therefore does not emerge merely to "fill in the gaps" in scientific knowledge. It emerges to grasp as object for the subject the cosmic domain of which the subject perceives herself as a manifestation, prior to the objectifying activity of the brain, and wherein her engagement with the world drawsits meaning.

CHAPTER V:
METADATA MODEL

Possibility theory and artificial intelligence

Over the last decade of the writing of this book the development of computer tools for decision making has taken an enormous step. The technology of machine learning, in a form called "artificial intelligence" based on iterative "neural networks," has developed routines that can simulate, and thereby supplement or even replace, human decision making in complex areas of cognitive activity, including medicine.

These tools are programmed to harvest artifacts of human thought and creative praxis for their manifest and latent content and patterns, and to reconstitute from them emergent language strings and aesthetic products thatsimulate the output of a conscious agent. So good is this computational analysis that its output appears more sophisticated than even the human agent can produce.

These products emerge as if constituted *de novo* from conscious activity. An iterative process ensues from the neural networks that reconstitutes, then reappropriates, latent patterns found within human artifacts, such that itsproducts appear as if they are derived from the same creative response that is characteristic of consciousness, only better: a depth of 3-D in art never before seen in human drawing; empathy in a synthetic voice that is authentic and persuasive; poetry conjuring emotional intelligence; harmony and rhythm in jazz composition reproducing seasoned technique; the finding of common elements linking different human languages, even in lieu of established linguistic theory. This is a "harvesting and reappropriating" of which we alone are not capable.

In fact, in this simulation of human intelligence, the machine appears autonomously to develop intentionality, even to apply value-laden features of thought, with the ability to create and follow human-like goals.

Unlike the evolved brain however, AI in the form of the neural networks is an insular process. It is not a conduit whereby the cosmos comes to know itself. It does not perceive or have access to the infinite domain of cosmic possibility as a common source for dialogue, or as a course-correcting arbiter of truth - except in that these persist as remnants in the artifacts of human knowledge that it harvests. Therefore, it cannot create *de novo*, to develop ideas and value judgements in response to the domain of open-ended possibility. All apparent emergent activity in AI derives from the mining of latent patterns inherent in human artifact. Furthermore, as it grows from analysis of its own products, it becomes susceptible to encasement in its own consanguinity.

That is, it has no way to "shift data," from established paradigms that it already has harvested, to those of new paradigms by creating them in response to perception of possibility, nor harnessing a metaphor-creating capacity to grasp possibility newly as objects for the subject.

For AI, data are harvested from human artifact. New tokens emerge as derivative from these data, and are thus limited to the bounds of the paradigms in terms of which they already are defined as data. The harvesting of new data from additional human artifacts does not produce data *de novo* in the same way as human consciousness, responsive to the cosmic domain of possibility in which it partakes, and that it apprehends as its milieu.

For instance, a recent developer of microchips for AI proposed that, to protect emergent tokens from error, calculation at a fundamental level should be "based on the laws of physics," presumably because this is taken to represent the elements of reality. But what if this were Newtonian physics? Would the emergent process of AI proceed from there, on its own, to derive the theorems of general relativity and the standard model of quantum physics as its new foundation, and, beyond this, would it discover all the new theories of physics that have yet to emerge - or does this kind of scientific creativity, these "paradigm shifts," require access to the truth-tempering domain of cosmic possibility to which only organic consciousness has access?

Similarly, from AI models trained only on Bach and Mozart would music of Beethoven or of Shostakovich emerge? Or does this require familiarity with the "joy" of humanistic hope as evoked by the Enlightenment, or of existential "fear" as evoked by state totalitarianism, that these new musical forms emerged historically to elicit and engage? What of all the musical forms that have yet to emerge? What would need to inform AI for them? Would mere user "prompts" suffice to generate them, or would the AI system somehow first have to experience the cosmic domain of open-ended possibility, as made possible through the evolved brain as qualia?

Would an AI diagnostic tool that discovers gender to be a risk factor for a certain disease have been able to do so if not first given the notions of "gender," "risk factor," "disease," "diagnosis," and "statistical analysis" by the programmer, each an anthropic product of centuries of creative paradigm development in the areas of medicine and epistemology? For our time, can AI, on its own, shift away from the modern notion of a "diagnosis," as a distinct discoverable entity of disease defined in terms of current physiologic paradigms, and to a notion instead of health and illness manifesting as "phenotype?" Will we be using the terminology of old paradigms derived from AI harvesting when we make such a paradigm shift to molecular biology?

That is, does AI "know" to account for the inherent limitation of notions such as "diagnosis," as they serve as metaphorical tools, because it senses the cosmic domain of possibility to which the term is accountable? Does it know how to respond creatively to a domain of possibility? Does it know to engage the user, in lieu of this awareness, to accommodate for its own deficit?

If AI calculation were to perform as if it were aware that access to the domain of possibility is essential for emergence, then its constitutive process would have to manifest as an engagement with the conscious user, as the source of this essential modulating input.

But this awareness would require AI neural networks

first to have discovered this notion itself within the mined artifacts of human knowledge that it harvests. But, if human thought is by its nature oblivious to this feature of cognition, then so will be the human artifacts upon which AI neural networks are based.

For instance, if we ourselves mistake "calculation" as sufficient for human cognition, and do not recognize a cosmic domain to which knowledge responds creatively, then our AI tools also will not know to look outside its own iterative process.

The role of a metadata model

Therefore, to create a model for computer decision support that facilitates medical decision making, we must take a focus very different from AI. Rather than analyzing linguistic string patterns and other products of praxis for latent patterns, we must consider the origin and role of "data" as epistemological artifacts, created in response to the perception of open-ended possibility.

Our theory of decision making therefore will take the form of a "metadata model" that is based on possibility theory and metaphor induction, and that is designed to facilitate the subject's creative response to the direct apprehension of possibility in consciousness.

In this model there does remain a role for AI, as a real-time source of established paradigms, that once were forged in the creative context of consciousness. AI cannot itself respond to possibility, but an AI agent can be fashioned, in terms of the "discovery" myth, to make available to the decision-maker a repository of these well-formed metaphors, as we will discuss below.

A metadata model is a theory of the origin and role of data-as-data in the decision-making process. It is unaffected by data content or real-world application. Instead, it reduces all data, regardless of content or application, to a common set of elements that account for their function as data in every instance of decision-making. With this model one can design algorithms with which to build computer decision tools that are applicable in all data-based situations.

Thereby the metadata model also serves to make tangible the elemental features of decision making - in our case, the metaphorical grasp and actualization of human possibility. This makes explicit the creative process of medical decision making, and it sheds light on the agenda of medicine as a humanistic project.

The origin of the "evidence-based" model

The hypnotic feature of metaphor induction causes data to appear discovered as given, and their logical relations to appear inherent to the data. Thereby data do not appear to the user as a volitional metaphorical grasp of possibility, but as the grasped possibility itself.

As a result, data are taken by modern medicine to be the basic elements of the medical decision, and their logical necessity as the necessary truth of the derived therapeutic formulations.

This illusion is the origin of the model of medical decision making called "evidence-based medicine." In terms of this model, the foundation of medical decision making appears to consist of data serving as the given predicates of a logical argument - that is, decision making appears to be essentially "evidence-based."

Evidence-based medicine treats data and their logical relations as the fundamental elements of the medicaldecision. Decision making is presumed to entail nothing but a rigorous observation of given data and fidelity to their inherent logical relations. The creative hand of the decision-maker in building this coherent formulation, in response to possibility, remains occult.

Computer algorithms based on this metadata model are designed to facilitate data discovery and retrieval, as the absolute beginning and end of the medical decision. The role of the clinician is reduced to clerical data entry and retrieval. The given data and their logical necessity as formulated are presumed to be sufficient to generate the correct decision on behalf of the clinician.

Historically the computer database structure that best accommodated this evidence-based model was called a "relational database." In a relational database, data are stored directly in the form in which they appear to be given, since they are taken to refer to nothing but themselves as the intended ends, and since their storage and retrieval are taken to be the beginning and the end ofthe medical decision process.

Thus, data are stored in the form of distinct tables, each taking the name of the class of the given data that it stores, such as "Patients" or "Diagnoses" or "Test Results." The logical relations between these data, such as the mapping of specific diagnoses to specific patients, also are stored in these tables. The result is a "relational database."

Illustration of an evidence-based system

A depiction of a typical relational database that one might find used in medicine is as below. Data are stored in the backend in distinct tables, each named after the data category. The front-end user interface serves to prompt the user to store and to retrieve these data as they are given.

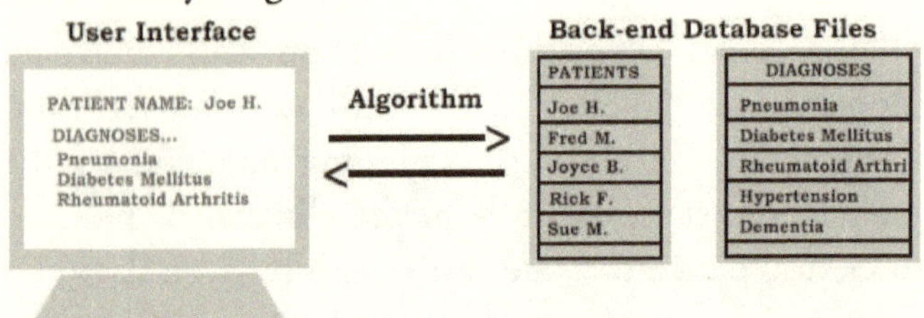

The coded algorithm above that intervenes between the front-end user interface and the backend data tables serves to facilitate this storage-and-retrieval process.

In this model, there is no representation of, and thus no provision made for, a creative process whereby data and their logical relations come into being in response to perception of possibility, as it is apprehended directly in the doctor-patient relationship. Because of this omission, and since the medical decision is, in fact, essentially a creative response, the clinician will experience such evidence-based tools as an obstacle rather than as an aid in decision-making.

Indeed, this has been the nature of the struggle of the first several decades of the computerization of medicine. Furthermore, such a relational database eventually becomes unwieldy and unmanageable; for as clinical needs and medical terms evolve over time, the structure of data tables and their logical relations must change continually.

Possibility theory as a metadata model

On the other hand, a metadata model that is based on possibility theory and metaphor induction treats data not as the given predicates of a logical system, but as intermediary artifacts of a creative response to perceived possibility, as it is apprehended directly in the doctor- patient relationship. Logical relations between data are created as ad hoc constructs whereby possibility is grasped for the sake of the subject-object interaction whereby possibility is actualized.

Therefore, the resulting data are not stored as given elements in static categorical tables, but as evolving content. The only "stationary" features of this model are the metaphor functions shared by all data, that do not change as the data content or their categories change.

This stationary structure can be represented by a single table, with columns that are named after these individual metaphor functions, as illustrated above.

As shown below, there still is a user front-end that prompts the storage and retrieval of backend data. But this process is driven by the clinician's creative response to open-ended possibility as it is perceived in the patient encounter.

Data are created to grasp possibility metaphorically, and thus they are stored and retrieved in terms of their metaphorical components, not as ends in themselves, and so not in their own terms.

There is one column for "root metaphors," and one column for emerging "submetaphors," as the categories of these root metaphors. And there is a third "inductions"column, wherein the user stores actionable metaphorical constructs, that are derived from the root metaphors and their submetaphors, and in terms of which possibility is grasped. Entire paradigm shifts can occur within thisstructure without modification of the background structure itself.

User Interface

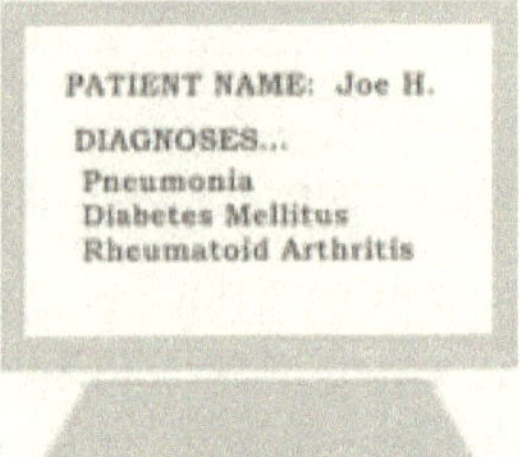

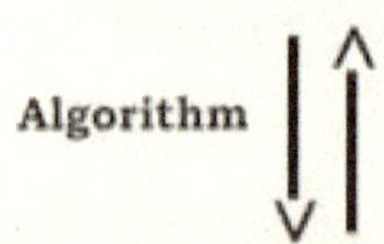

Algorithm

Back-end Database File

PARADIGM	ROOT-METAPHORS	SUB-METAPHORS	INDUCTIONS
Patients	John Doe	Age	65
Patients	John Doe	Symptom	Fever
Patients	Sally Smith	Appointment	1/23/2010
Diagnoses	Pneumonia	Symptom	Cough
Diagnoses	Pneumonia	Treatment	Antibiotic
Diagnoses	Lupus	Test	ANA

The coded algorithm that intervenes between the user interface and the backend database are designed not to anticipate "given" data, but to anticipate the need for a creative response to open-ended possibility, as it is encountered in the doctor-patient relationship.

The algorithm facilitates the clinician's creative response to this horizon of possibility. Data emerge metaphorically, and these components are stored as transient metaphorical products. Their on-going modification and retrieval serve to grasp human possibility in the form of objects, thereby to precipitate the subject-object interaction whereby human possibilityis actualized.

Such a database tool does not presume to lead the clinician to a foregone conclusion. It cannot serve this role because it does not perceive possibility, and so cannot itself respond to possibility. Rather, it is designed to facilitate the clinician's perception of and creative response to possibility.

Harnessing the "discovery" myth

The hallmark of a well-designed computer tool is that it is invisible to the user. It should not represent a new project over which the subject stumbles. Like a well- designed pair of glasses, if the tool is well-conceived, the user will see only the intended object of her gaze when the tool is applied.

Therefore, to design an effective computer tool the designer must "get into the head" of the computer user. The designer must appreciate that data, even as they emerge as created products with which to grasp open-ended possibility, still must appear to the user as if they are "discovered," that is, as the grasped possibility itself. Only in this way does the subject-object interaction eruptwhereby possibility is actualized.

Toward this purpose the algorithm should harness thelanguage of "discovery" as a myth.

For example, to grasp therapeutic possibilities in a particular ill patient in a gestalt fashion, the interface might offer up a set of diagnostic root metaphors from which to choose. But it must do this by asking the user "which of these diagnoses does the patient have?" Thereby it camouflages a creative choice of metaphor as an act of "discovery."

Such a system cannot anticipate every metaphor that might be useful in grasping an infinite range of clinical possibility. But it can anticipate the open-ended natureof that possibility, and it can facilitate the creation of new metaphorical terms with which to grasp possibility.

In this way the backend structure of a database that is based on metaphor induction does not have to change. Its set of metaphorical functions serve to accommodate any and all cases of creative response to possibility.

For instance, in addition to new "diagnostic" entities, new perspectives on patient care can be accommodated under the rubric of possibility, such as "palliative" care, or emerging social projects for the community, such as "population screening," as in the case of an epidemic or climate change, or the coordination of care with other community resources, such as shelters or food banks.

In this way, a computer decision tool based on possibility theory can serve the more fundamental social agenda of medicine, of which the clinical decision is an instance and a paradigm.

Example of an AI agent

It is not the purpose of this book to explore a role for "artificial intelligence" in medical decision making. In time, machine learning will be just another programming tool for the design of software to assist medicine in its more fundamental role in the actualization of human possibility. The purpose of this book has been only to explore the social agenda of medicine.

However, looking at artificial intelligence is useful for this deeper purpose. The presumption that artificial intelligence not only can "simulate," but can "supplant" medical decision making forces an exploration of those features of medical decision making that, in fact, cannot be reproduced by AI. This helps to elucidate the features of medical decision making that rely on consciousness.

Thus, it is helpful to imagine an AI application (in the form of an interactive "agent") that truly assists medical decision making. This serves to distinguish the boundary that separates machine learning from human cognition.

Medical decision making, in every instance, begins with subjective awareness of failure of expected human possibility - conceived of as an "illness." This subjective impression then precipitates a metaphorical grasp of this failed human possibility, as a "symptom" or a "finding," such as "fever," or "rash," or "headache," so that it then can be intended as an object for resolution - in terms of "cure," or a return to "health."

Toward this end, the mind seeks for a paradigm of pathophysiology, serving as a unifying root metaphor, interms of which this objective finding gains contextual meaning, and with which objective measurements and therapeutic intervention can be fashioned. This creative urge to apply a unifying root metaphor is experienced bythe clinician as an impulse to "discover" the diagnosis.

An AI agent, using this same "discovery" rubric, can present to the clinician various diagnostic options, called the "differential diagnosis," from which the clinician can choose. These interactive considerations (looking at the terminology of diagnoses as they apply to the patient) serve to introduce established metaphorical frameworks, with which to further explore, and to objectively grasp and actualize, perceived human possibility. Thereby, the AI agent empowers the medical decision.

In this example, the AI agent is seen to facilitate, without interfering with, the clinician's creative responseto perceived human possibility.

In contrast, if the AI agent were designed instead to "determine the diagnosis" by itself, on behalf of the clinician, then the creative process of responding to perceived human possibility would be aborted. The diagnosis would be mistaken as the end in itself, rather than as a means to this deeper end. It would lose access to the domain of possibility as arbiter of its formulation and clinical application. Machine learning, as artificial intelligence, can simulate this creative human response, but it cannot reproduce it, because it does not perceive possibility as does the evolved human brain.

An understanding of the central role of perception of possibility in medical decision making is essential for the proper design and use of a machine learning tool, including making sure that it stays within its lane.

Medicine as social science

Our metadata model, based on possibility theory and metaphor induction, displays the creative process of medical decision making. It demonstrates that medicine essentially is a social science that uses the physical sciences creatively for its deeper human agenda. This human agenda is the perception of possibility for the sake of its actualization. The objective data and logical coherence of medical decision making come into beingas artifacts of this creative response.

Empathy, as perception of possibility in the other, is the milieu of the doctor-patient relationship. The courage of the physician to respond to open-ended possibility is an instance of, and a paradigm for, the social agenda of medicine. The social agenda of medicine is the creative response to open-ended possibility as the ground of the human condition. For this reason, medicine exists as a necessary social institution in every time and place. It is the sanctuary for the courageous response of mankind, totake uncertainty upon itself as the human condition.

APPENDIX A

Possibility

The purpose of this book has been to describe the agenda of medicine as a social institution, and to describe how the medical decision emerges to serve it. Our ultimate goal is to empower medicine by returning it to its humanistic foundation, in bedside practice andits broader anthropologic role and responsibility.

Possibility and Physician. *Susan Saandholland on Midjourney*

As our argument developed, it entailed describing the human condition, the existential context of medical practice, as open-ended possibility, and describing the objective medical decision as a creative response to the subjective perception of human possibility. This overall ontological framework for the medical ethic, thus called "possibility theory," portrayed the social agenda of medicine as the actualization of human possibility.

In review, I have introduced six conclusions below, developed in the course of this book, along with their corollary notions, selected here because they recreate the overall philosophical narrative.

1. The brain is the source of consciousness.

All of our observations - experimental, clinical, and pedestrian - point to this material foundation. A reliable correlation is observed between accidental or intentional abruption of brain matter and an alteration of behavioror of subjective awareness. Even if consciousness is an emerging feature of the cosmos, separate from the brain, it nevertheless requires the brain for its emergence.

The problem with moving from this observation, tocreating a science of consciousness, and that has been called the "hard problem of consciousness" by David Chalmers, is the difference between the experience of a material world, on the one hand, and the experience of experiencing a material world, on the other - that is, the awareness of awareness, or of consciousness itself.

This difference in kind of experience has suggestedto some the existence of distinct fundamental substances for each experience ("mind" versus "matter"). It is this difference in kind that blocks a theoretical formulation of a causal link, from its beginning to the end. This results in what has been called the "explanatory gap" in the parlance of modern science.

Normally, modern science would seek to reduce consciousness, as it does for all objects of investigation, to a series of material links in causation, progressing in this case from initial physical loci or processes in the brain, to a final targeted conscious event.

But this final targeted event, by definition, is measurable only subjectively. It has its existence only in the mind. Thus, this final causal link is impossible to construct in material terms. Additionally, coming at this hard problem from a different angle: If objective links are "products" of consciousness, that is, if consciousness is a pre-objective field that is the source of objects in the mind, then it would be paradoxical, and impossible, to reduce consciousness to them - to its own products.

It is true that correlations between regions of the brain and specific features of consciousness, called the "correlates of consciousness" by researchers such as Francis Crick and Christof Koch, have utilitarian value for medical research and clinical management. But a science of material causality of consciousness itself, from a material beginning to a targeted subjective end, remains out of reach, possibly awaiting a reassessment of the role and nature of "material" vis-a-vis the mind - possibly a material theory of the origin of material-formulations themselves in consciousness, that thereby acknowledges a self-referential limitation, and closes the explanatory gap.

2. The brain, though necessary for consciousness, is not the sufficient, "insular" source of consciousness.

In that the brain is an evolved constituent of the universe, and that the content of consciousness (the things we think about) are features of the universe, the brain is just that organ through which the universe has come to know itself.

A good analogy for the brain then is the transistor radio. The radio is necessary for creating the sound that is emitted from it. The sound, as sound, does not exist without the function of the radio. But the radio is not sufficient for the production of sound. The radio serves as a conduit through which electro-magnetic waves are reconstituted as sound.

Similarly, the brain has evolved as a "conduit" of sorts, through which the universe, possibly in the form of cosmic waves or of quantum events, is reconstituted as the subjective experience of cosmic "self-knowing." This appears as individual consciousness, and it takes the form, in the theater of the mind, of an objective world set apart from a subjective knower.

Thus, these two apparent substances, "matter and mind," are in fact manifestations of a common source, now bifurcated into two interactive features in the mind. The objective world and the subjective knower each isan aspect of the one universe, the one requiring the other for its existence in the constituted theater of the mind.

An organic connection between brain and cosmos is necessary for the emergence of consciousness. Just as the chlorophyll-containing leaves of a plant absorb the sun at a quantum level to convert sunlight into sugar, so the brain has evolved to conjoin with, or to take in, the cosmos at some fundamental level for the emergence of consciousness.

Therefore, consciousness is not a mere product of insular "calculation," that can be reproduced by another calculator substrate. It is the artifact of an organ evolvedto conjoin with the cosmos as a conduit. A machine can do this if designed to so conjoin with the universe. But thus far the only such machine is the evolved brain.

The substance of consciousness therefore is not the physical material of the brain, and it will not be found by looking therein at gray matter. The substance of consciousness is the cosmos itself, manifesting through the agency of the brain, and in the limited anthropic waythat the brain makes possible.

3. What we call the material, or physical, does not represent the limits of reality, but the limits of knowing of reality through the evolved brain.

Even our observation of the physical brain itself isa reconstitution by the brain for our consciousness. As Bertrand Russell said, "What the physiologist sees whenhe examines a brain is in the physiologist, not in the brain he is examining."

This does not mean that what appears as matter is actually mental. We are not here proposing an idealistic ontology. It means simply that the notion of mind versus matter, or of an "internal" versus "external" world, are mythologic constructs, fabricated to accommodate a bifurcated reconstitution of the cosmos by the brain.

It just makes practical sense that the brain, being always incompletely evolved, manifests such limits in reconstituting what we perceive as the world. As Arthur Eddington said, "It would be unreasonable to limit our thought of nature to what can be comprised in sense-pictures." [54]

As a corollary, in consciousness we are aware of a pre-objective background domain, of which the object, and the knower, are manifestations. There is something "behind the veil" that we know to be the source of what we call self and world. This is the domain that we hereinhave identified as infinite possibility.

The imperfect apposition of an evolved mind with the infinite background world that it intends, manifests for instance when the rubric of interactive "molecules" of molecular biology requires additional positing of an epi-genome, or when an attempt to grasp the cosmos as "objects," in the form of particles or waves, results in a measurement problem, wherein the object itself is said to change with observation (the "collapse" of the wave), when, in fact, any object, as such, is insufficient to grasp a cosmos that must consist of object and subject unified.

4. Objective knowledge is a product of the creative response to subjective perception of possibility.

What we call objective knowledge comes into being through the projection of metaphor onto perceived possibility, to grasp it as an "object" for the subject in mind, so that through the resulting subject-object interaction, intended possibility is actualized. This is theorigin and the goal of objective knowledge.

The interactive process is experienced as the myth of "objective science," wherein objective formulations, though created, appear discovered as given. The illusion of a created object as given induces the subject-object interaction whereby possibility (in which both subject and object partake) is actualized.

This mythologic perspective permits a unification of mystical insight with the scientific agenda. When we recognize the steps through which objective knowledge emerges from subjective perception of possibility, their interdependent connection becomes clear. The mystical perception of possibility is no longer "mysterious," but is recognized as part of the natural process of knowing.

From this, one then can argue that the presence of the possibility-perceiving physician at the patient's bedside is just as necessary for a medical decision as is an objective test result; for it is perception of human possibility that determines what test result will be called "disease," indeed for what will be called a "test."

That which we call "natural" in the natural sciences is preferred to the mystical, not because it is a guarantor of truth, but because it is a guarantor of responsibility for our decisions, by making the elements of our decision explicit. But the "mystical" insight, being perception of possibility, also is necessary, to bring form and substance to the objective medical decision.

Thus, the study of the language of medicine is the study of a myth, whose basic form in every era is "health versus illness." By grasping human possibility inthe negative as "illness," as it is formulated in terms of the pathophysiology of an era, the mind is directed to itsactualization as "health," formulated in these same terms, serving as the tools of actualization. Thus, the structure and function of the myth remains constant over time, even as paradigms of pathophysiology change.

To call a language system a myth is not to make a judgement regarding its truth or falsity, but to focus on its utility for the user. In our case, this utility lies in the grasp and actualization of human possibility.

The terms that accomplish this are the terms of "discovery." Discovery is that moment when the art and the science of medicine come together. That is, it occurs when the creative metaphorical grasp of possibility as anobject is experienced as "finding" this object as given.

Herein, the terms of discovery serve as a myth. For instance, the challenge to "discover" prompts a creative grasp of possibility as an object. The extended language of discovery serves to further execute this process. For instance, the notion of discovery implicates a domain of "reality," as a reified repository wherein objects that willbe discovered are said to preexist. Objects are said to be discovered "in reality."

The "reality" myth functions in his way: The nature of reality itself is defined ahead of time, in ad hoc terms, so that objects formulated as found therein take on thesesame characteristics. Thus, when Bertrand Russell asks, "How do we know about the physical world?," he is begging the question of a "physical" reality, in terms of which objects of the world will be discovered.

This myth of "discovery," as it is not aware of itselfas myth, does not acknowledge the ground in possibility that it serves.

Therefore, for instance, this ground of possibility remains invisible to the theory of evolution, even as stochasticity is the driving mechanism whereby cosmic possibility comes into being. The neo-Darwinian myth describes this manifestation into actuality as the result ofthe "conditions of competition." As these conditions are formulated as discovered as given, their mythological role in the grasp of possibility is obscured. Thus, that which comes into being is presumed to be meaningless by virtue of a "random" ground of competition.

But it is the ground of possibility that gives meaning to emerging actuality; for all that is, is actual only because it is possible. It is the infinite domain of possibility, not perspectival competition, that determinesthe structure of actuality.

5. Perception of possibility is the fundamental level of consciousness.

To restate this in a way that is more consistent withour developing theory: Perception of possibility is the mode in which the universe first is aware of itself through the agency of the evolved brain. Perception of possibility distinguishes human from machine learning, for a machine, as machine, cannot perceive the cosmic domain of open-ended possibility.

Of course, the term "possibility" is a metaphor.

And, as with all metaphors, it serves an anthropic end. In this instance, it emerges to accommodate the fact that the cosmos first is perceived as a predicate to its own actualization. Thus, we say that the cosmos is perceived as a domain of "possibility." As Schopenhauer said, in retort to Leibniz' assertion that the actual world is the "best of all possible worlds," if God created the world, then he created possibility. The cosmos first perceives its own nature, through the agency of the evolved brain, as a domain of possibility.

Thus, we speak of the fundamental laws of nature as underlying all that is, or that might be, actual; we argue that a proposition might be true, or cannot be true, based upon whether we perceive it to be possible; we assess scientific theory based on possible outcome; we acknowledge truth in the Beatitudes of Jesus because we recognize the possibility affirmed therein, regardless of their actuality in the present. That is, we perceive the universe fundamentally as a domain of possibility.

This sets the stage to describe the human condition in terms of open-ended possibility, and to see theory as serving this end.

Thus, for example, "empathy," conceived of as perception of possibility in the other, is fundamental to the medical decision. The medical decision is the fashioning of objective terms of pathophysiology for the grasp and actualization of human possibility. This is the agenda of the individual medical decision, and so of medicine as a social institution, of which the medical decision is an instance and a paradigm.

The technical work of this monograph lies in

describing the creative steps through which an objective theory arises from subjective impression of possibility. This is necessary in order to demonstrate that objective theory is an artifact, a product, of subjective impression, and thereby to rescue medicine from the illusion that theobjective medical decision is the given end in itself.

6. The essence of the human self is its emergence as the self-knowing aspect of the universe.

Therein, open-ended possibility defines the human condition. Coming to grips with this is the human dilemma. There is no foundation of physical or social law other than its utility in the grasp and actualization ofpossibility. There is no moral foundation other than responsibility for what is actualized. What we call the experience of "beauty" is the recognition of possibility manifesting as actuality. This is why a mathematical formula can be said to be beautiful. What we call "art" isevocation of possibility for its own sake for the viewer.

As perception of possibility, consciousness is its own vindication; for it is the self in the act of attending to that for which it has come into being. What we call the "other" is recognition of the universe manifesting as self-knowing. Thus, when we engage with the other, we are engaging the universe. This is why engagement with the other always has moral significance and formative ramification for the knower. Altruism is self-interest, not because it "comes around also to help us in the end" or as an artifact of "natural selection" at a community scale, but because perception of the other is a predicate to becoming fully human. We are less human if we do not do this. This is Aristotle's assertion that the "good" is simply that which a good "human" does.

Perception of possibility thus creates the agenda of medicine, the foundation of medical ethics, and the creative origin of medical science.

The postmodern philosophers of the 20th century mistook the significance of material reductionism, to proclaim the "death of the self." This imagined locus of thought was presumed to be a phantom, an illusion of a material brain, not an emergent real being that stands independently as a source of human value.

But, as the brain creates the conditions of cosmic self-awareness, the self is simply the brain's perception of this instantiation of cosmic self-awareness. So, the self has existence, even if fleeting with the brain, no less than does the eternal universe that it manifests. In this, its substance is rightly perceived to be eternal. As Spinoza said, "If we pay attention to the common opinion of men, we shall see that they are conscious of the eternity of their minds; but they confuse eternity with duration..."

Eternity, as it is perceived in ourselves and in the other, is the focus of the practice of medicine. It is participation in the infinite domain of possibility as it manifests as humanity. This is what we grieve, in illness and in death, as it is what we love as ourselves and in the other. Anything that interferes with this is made into "disease," for its address at the hand of the medical decision. In this also is the agenda of medicine as a social institution.

FOOTNOTES

[1]. Nagel, T., Mind and Cosmos, (New York: Oxford University Press, 2012), p. 61.

[2]. Sagan, Carl, YouTube video, Title: Carl Sagan – ProfoundWords of Wisdom, from the television series Cosmos; broadcast in 1980; Episode: The Shores of the Cosmic Ocean; Sagan delivers the line during an introductory speech near the beginning of episode. (https://youtu.be/wLigBYhdUDs?t=141)

[3]. Eddington, A. S., The Nature of the Physical World, (New York: The Macmillan Company, 1929), p. 267. (public domain)

[4]. Eddington, A. S., The Philosophy of Physical Science, (New York: Cambridge University Press, 1939), p 207.

[5]. Rilke, Rainer Maria. "Wenn es nur einmal.../If only for once..." by Reiner Maria Rilke, copyright 1996 by Anita Barrows and Joanna Macy; from RILKE'S BOOK OF HOURS by Rainer Maria Rilke, translated by Anita Barrowsand Joanna Macy. Used by permission of Riverhead, an imprint of Penguin Publishing Group, a division of Penguin Random House LLC. All rights reserved. p. 53.

[6]. Eddington, A. S., The Nature of the Physical World, (NewYork: The Macmillan Company, 1929), p 331. (public domain)

[7]. Cobb, M., Life's Greatest Secret: The Race to Crack

the Genetic Code, (New York: Basic Books, 2015), p 313.

[8]. Light, J., Pillemer, D., Summing Up: The Science of Reviewing Research, (Cambridge: Harvard University Press,1984), p. 105.

[9]. Tillich, P., "The Religious Symbol," in Symbolism in Religion and Literature, ed. Rollo May (London: ForgottenBooks, 2017), p 88.

[10]. Eddington, A. S., The Mathematical Theory of Relativity, (Cambridge: Cambridge University Press, 1923), p.5. (public domain)

[11]. Tillich, P., The Courage To Be, (New Haven: Yale University Press, 1980), p. 88.

[12]. Eddington, A. S., The Mathematical Theory of Relativity, (Cambridge: Cambridge University Press, 1923), p.219. (public domain)

[13]. Tillich, P., Systematic Theology Vol III, (Chicago: TheUniversity of Chicago Press, 1971), p 75.

[14]. Eddington, A. S., Space Time and Gravitation: An Outline of the General Relativity Theory, (New York: Cambridge University Press, 1920), p 30. (public domain -published before 1923)

[15]. Eddington, A. S., The Nature of the Physical World, (New York: The Macmillan Company, 1929), p 248. (publicdomain)

[16]. Eddington, A. S., The Nature of the Physical World,(New York: The Macmillan Company, 1929), p

281-282.(public domain)

[17]. Heidegger, M., Being and Time, translated by Macquarrie, J. and Robinson, E., (San Francisco: HarperCollins, 1962), chp 7, p 38.

[18]. Eddington, A. S., Space Time and Gravitation: An Outline of the General Relativity Theory, (New York: Cambridge University Press, 1920), p 46. (public domain -published before 1923)

[19]. Plato, Collected Dialogues: Timaeus, ed. Hamilton, K.,Cairns, H., (Princeton University Press, 1978), p. 1167.

[20]. Capra, F., The Tao of Physics, (Boston: Shambhala Publications, Inc., 2010), p. 154.

[21]. Capra, F., The Tao of Physics, (Boston: Shambhala Publications, Inc., 2010), pp. 150-171.

[22]. Capra, F., The Tao of Physics, (Boston: Shambhala Publications, Inc., 2010), pp. 212-222.

[23]. Eddington, A. S., The Nature of the Physical World, (New York: The Macmillan Company, 1929), p 330. (publicdomain)

[24]. Eddington, A. S., The Nature of the Physical World, (New York: The Macmillan Company, 1929), p 321. (publicdomain)

[25]. Tillich, P., The Eternal Now, (New York: Charles Scribner's Sons, 1963), chp III, p. 45

[26]. Hippocrates, The Nature of Man, translated by

Jones, W.H.S., (Cambridge: Harvard University Press, 1959), p. 11.(online)

[27]. Harris, H., The Birth of the Cell, (New Haven: YaleUniversity Press, 1999), p. 29.

[28]. Margulies, A., "Toward Empathy: The Uses of Wonder," The American Journal of Psychiatry 141:9 (1984), 1025-1033; p. 1029.

[29]. Polanyi, M., The Tacit Dimension (Garden City, NY:Doubleday and Company, 1967), p. 80.

[30]. Goldstein, J., Brown, M., Harrison's Principles of Internal Medicine 12th edition, ed. Wilson, J. D. (McGraw-Hill, 1991), p. 21.

[31]. Gelehrter, T., King, R., Ledbetter, D., Nussbaum, R., Genetics and Molecular Medicine in Medical Knowledge Self Assessment IX (USA: American College of Physicians, 1991),p. 20.

[32]. Bayrak-Toydemir, P., et al, "Hereditary hemorrhagic telangiectasia: An overview of diagnosis and management in the molecular era for clinicians," Genetics in Medicine, vol 6:number 4 (July/Aug 2004), 175-191; p. 175.

[33]. Eddington, A. S., The Philosophy of Physical Science, (New York: Cambridge University Press, 1939), p 111.

[34]. Eddington, A. S., Space Time and Gravitation: An Outline of the General Relativity Theory, (New York: Cambridge University Press, 1920), p 182.

(public domain -published before 1923)

[35]. Eddington, A. S., The Philosophy of Physical Science, (New York: Cambridge University Press, 1939), pp 21, 114-115.

[36]. Eddington, A. S., The Philosophy of Physical Science, (New York: Cambridge University Press, 1939), pp. 104, 122.

[37]. Eddington, A. S., The Philosophy of Physical Science, (New York: Cambridge University Press, 1939), p. 181.

[38]. Eddington, A. S., The Philosophy of Physical Science, (New York: Cambridge University Press, 1939), p. 104.

[39]. Heisenberg, W., Physics and Philosophy, (New York,Harper Torchbooks, 1958), p 58.

[40]. Eddington, A. S., The Philosophy of Physical Science, (New York: Cambridge University Press, 1939), pp. 85-90.

[41]. Marcus Aurelius Antoninus, Meditations, translated byFarquharson, A.S.L. (New York, Alfred A. Knopf, 1992).

[42]. Eddington, A. S., The Philosophy of Physical Science, (New York: Cambridge University Press, 1939), p. 111

[43]. Planck, M., Scientific Autobiography and Other Papers, (Westport, Connecticut: Greenwood Press, 1971), p 58-59.

[44]. Bohr, N., Atomic Physics and the Description of Nature,(New York: John Wiley & sons, 1958), p. 57.

[45]. Burns, G., The Science of Genetics: An Introduction to Heredity, (New York: Macmillan Publishing, 1983), p. 3-4.

[46]. Johannsen W. Elemente der exakten Erblichkeitslehre, (Jena: Gustav Fischer, 1909), quote translated by Nils Roll- Hansen in "The holist tradition in twentieth century genetics. Wilhelm Johannsen's genotype concept", The Journal of Physiology 2014 Jun 1; 592(Pt 11): 2431-2438; (online: https://www.ncbi.nlm.nih.gov/pmc/articles/PMC4048101)

[47]. Schrodinger, E. What is Life?, (London, CambridgeUniversity Press, 2001), pp. 24, 55, 84.

[48]. Cobb, M., Life's Greatest Secret: The Race to Crack the Genetic Code, (New York: Basic Books, 2015), p 159.

[49]. Eddington, A. S., The Philosophy of Physical Science, (New York: Cambridge University Press, 1939), p. 111

[50]. Polya, G., How To Solve It, (Princeton, NJ: PrincetonUniversity Press, 1945), p. 75

[51]. James, W., The Sentiment of Rationality, (Andesite Press, 2015)

[52]. Eddington, A. S., The Philosophy of Physical Science, (New York: Cambridge University Press, 1939), p. 147

[53]. Davies, P., The Origin of Life, (London: Penguin Books,2003), p. 43.

[54]. Eddington, A. S., Space Time and Gravitation: An Outline of the General Relativity Theory, (New York: Cambridge University Press, 1920), p 29. (public domain -published before 1923)

[55]. Bohm, D., Hiley, B., "On the Intuitive Understanding ofNonlocality as Implied by Quantum Theory" in Foundations of Physics vol 5:issue 1 (Mar 1975), 93-109; pp. 96, 102.

[56]. Eddington, A. S., The Philosophy of Physical Science, (New York: Cambridge University Press, 1939), p. 61

[57]. Davies, P., The Origin of Life, (London: Penguin Books,2003), p. 252.

[58]. Nagel, T., Mind and Cosmos, (New York: Oxford University Press, 2012), pp. 105-107.

[59]. Nagel, T., Mind and Cosmos, (New York: Oxford University Press, 2012), p. 85.

[60]. Dressler, A., Voyage to the Great Attractor , (New York:Knopf Doubleday, 1994), p. 335.

[61]. Eddington, A. S., The Philosophy of Physical Science, (New York: Cambridge University Press, 1939), p. 150.

[62]. Eddington, A. S., The Philosophy of Physical Science, (New York: Cambridge University Press, 1939), p. 69

[63]. Planck, M., quoted in The Observer, London, (Jan 25,1931).

[64]. Russell, B., Analysis of Matter, (Nottingham, England:Spokesman Books, 2007), p. 320.

[65]. Raman, V. V., "Four Perspectives on Consciousness" in Quantum Physics of Consciousness vol 14, edited by Penrose,R., Hameroff, S. (Cambridge: Cosmology Science Publishers,2011), p. 92.

[66]. Eddington, A. S., Space Time and Gravitation: An Outline of the General Relativity Theory, (New York: Cambridge University Press, 1920), p 175. (public domain -published before 1923)

[67].Asvaghosha, The Awakening of Faith, introduction by Abe, R., translated by Hakeda, Y. S. (New York: ColumbiaUniversity Press, 2006), p. 8.

[68]. Hameroff S, Penrose R. Conscious events as orchestrated spacetime selections. Journal of Consciousness Studies 1996;3(1), 36-53.

[69]. Nagel, T., What is it like to be a bat?, The PhilosophicalReview 1974; 83:435-450.

[70]. Eddington, A. S., The Nature of the Physical World, (New York: The Macmillan Company, 1929), p 286. (publicdomain)

[71]. Frankl, V. E., Man's Search for Meaning, (Boston: Beacon Press, 1992), part 1, p. 33. online: http://www.fablar.in/yahoo_site_admin/assets/docs/Mans_Sea rch_for_Meaning.78114942.pdf

[72]. Marcus Aurelius Antoninus, Meditations, translated byFarquharson, A.S.L (New York, Everyman Library, 1992), pvi, 40.

[73]. Tillich, P., Systematic Theology Vol I, (Chicago: TheUniversity of Chicago Press, 1971), p 152.

[74]. Ortega y Gasset, J., The Revolt of the Masses, (NewYork: W.W. Nortaon and Company, 1960), pp. 33-34.

[75]. Nietzsche, F., The Will To Power, edited by Kaufmann,W., (New York: Random House, 1967), p. 35.

[76]. Nietzsche, F., The Will To Power, edited by Kaufmann, W., (New York: Random House, 1967), pp. 12-13.

[77]. Plato, Collected Dialogues: The Sophist, ed. Hamilton,K., Cairns, H., (Princeton University Press, 1978), p. 964.

[78]. Pepper, S., World Hypotheses, (Berkeley: University ofCalifornia Press, 1942), p. 91.

[79]. Eddington, A. S., The Philosophy of Physical Science, (New York: Cambridge University Press, 1939), p. 111

[80]. Capra, F., The Tao of Physics, (Boston: Shambhala Publications, Inc., 2010), p. 220.

[81]. Capra, F., The Tao of Physics, (Boston: Shambhala Publications, Inc., 2010), p. 161.

[82]. Toulmin, S., The Philosophy of Science, (New York:Harper and Row, 1960), p. 81.

[83]. Eddington, A. S., The Nature of the Physical World, (New York: The Macmillan Company, 1929), pp. 119-133.(public domain)

[84]. Internal Medicine Review Core Curriculum 16th edition, ed. Hannaman, R. A., (Colorado Springs: MedStudy Corporation, 2014), p. 2-1.

[85]. Plato, Collected Dialogues: Meno, ed. Hamilton, K., Cairns, H., (Princeton University Press, 1978), p. 365-370.

[86]. Capra, F., The Tao of Physics, (Boston: Shambhala Publications, Inc., 2010), p. 88.

[87]. Eddington, A. S., The Nature of the Physical World, (New York: The Macmillan Company, 1929), p. 305. (publicdomain)

[88]. Kline, M., Mathematics: The Loss of Certainty, (Oxford:Oxford University Press, 1982), pp. 12-13.

[89]. Capra, F., The Tao of Physics, (Boston: Shambhala Publications, Inc., 2010), p. 269.

[90]. Eddington, A. S., The Philosophy of Physical Science, (New York: Cambridge University Press, 1939), pp. 108-109.

[91]. Eddington, A. S., The Philosophy of Physical Science, (New York: Cambridge University Press, 1939), p. 114.

[92]. Eddington, A. S., The Philosophy of Physical Science, (New York: Cambridge University Press, 1939), p. 122.

[93]. Eddington, A. S., The Philosophy of Physical Science, (New York: Cambridge University Press, 1939), pp. 131-133.

[94]. Eddington, A. S., The Nature of the Physical World, (New York: The Macmillan Company, 1929), p. 244. (publicdomain)

[95]. Eddington, A. S., The Philosophy of Physical Science, (New York: Cambridge University Press, 1939), p. 17.

[96]. Eddington, A. S., The Nature of the Physical World, (New York: The Macmillan Company, 1929), pp. 241- 330.(public domain)

[97]. Eddington, A. S., The Philosophy of Physical Science, (New York: Cambridge University Press, 1939), p. 136.

[98]. Eddington, A. S., The Philosophy of Physical Science, (New York: Cambridge University Press, 1939), p. 181.

[99]. Eddington, A. S., The Philosophy of Physical Science, (New York: Cambridge MD Press, 1939), p. 111.

[100]. Eddington, A. S., The Philosophy of Physical Science, (New York: Cambridge University Press, 1939), p. 131.

[101]. Eddington, A. S., The Philosophy of Physical Science, (New York: Cambridge University Press, 1939), p. 131.

[102]. Kline, M., Mathematics: The Loss of Certainty, (Oxford: Oxford University Press, 1982), pp. 12.

[103]. Eddington, A. S., Space Time and Gravitation: An Outline of the General Relativity Theory, (New York: Cambridge University Press, 1920), p 12., quoting Bertrand Russell in Mysticism and Logic and other Essays (London:Longman, Green and Company, 1925), p. 27.

[104]. Eddington, A. S., The Philosophy of Physical Science, (New York: Cambridge University Press, 1939), p. 5.

[105]. Goldstein, J., Grown, M., Harrison's Principles of Internal Medicine 12th edition, ed. Wilson, J. D. (McGray-Hill, 1991), p. 23.

[106]. Eddington, A. S., The Philosophy of Physical Science, (New York: Cambridge University Press, 1939), p. 134.

[107]. Nietzsche, F., The Will To Power, edited by Kaufmann, W., (New York: Random House, 1967), p. 279

[108]. Hunter, G., Metalogic (Berkley: University of California Press, 1973), p. 93.

[109]. Eddington, A. S., The Mathematical Theory of Relativity, (Cambridge: Cambridge University Press,

1923), p. 105. (public domain)

[110]. Planck, M., Scientific Autobiography and Other Papers, (Westport, Connecticut: Greenwood Press, 1971), p 55.

[111]. Tillich, P., The Socialist Decision, translated by F. Sherman (New York, Harper & Row, Publishers, 1977), p 20.

[112]. Eddington, A. S., Space Time and Gravitation: An Outline of the General Relativity Theory, (New York: Cambridge University Press, 1920), p 46. (public domain -published before 1923)

[113]. Capra, F., The Tao of Physics, (Boston: ShambhalaPublications, Inc., 2010), p. 179.

[114]. Tillich, P., Systematic Theology Vol I, (Chicago: TheUniversity of Chicago Press, 1971), p 274.

[115]. Tillich, P., Systematic Theology Vol I, (Chicago: TheUniversity of Chicago Press, 1971), p 275.

[116]. Tillich, P., Systematic Theology Vol I, (Chicago: TheUniversity of Chicago Press, 1971), p 276.

[117]. Schweitzer, A., The Quest of the Historical Jesus, translated by W. Montgomery, J.R. Coates, S. Cupitt, J. Bowden (Minneapolis, Fortress Press, 2001), p 484.

[118]. Sartre, John-Paul, Being and Nothingness, translated by Barne, H., (New York: Washington Square Press, 1975), p. 159. (online edition: http://www.ahandfulofleaves.org/documents/BeingAndNothingness_Sartre.pdf. p. 107.)

[119]. James, W., The Varieties of Religious Experience (New York: Collier Books, 1961), p. 43. (quoting from Emerson, R. W., "Divinity School Address" 1838 at Divinity College, Cambridge, published in The Collected Works of Ralph Waldo Emerson (Cambridge: Harvard University Press, 1971), p. 77)

[120]. Sartre, John-Paul, Existentialism and Human Emotions (New York, Kensington Publishing Corp, 1985), p. 54.

[121]. Frankl, V. E., Man's Search for Meaning, (Boston: Beacon Press, 1992), part 1, p. 24. online: http://www.fablar.in/yahoo_site_admin/assets/docs/ Mans_Sea rch_for_Meaning.78114942.pdf

[122]. Denes, M., In Necessity and Sorrow (New York: BasicBooks, 1976), pp. 56-57.

[123]. Buber, M., I and Thou , trans. Smith, R. G., 2nd Englishedition, (Edinburgh: T. and T. Clark, 1987), p. 107.

[124]. Asvaghosha, The Awakening of Faith, introduction by Abe, R., translated by Hakeda, Y. S. (New York: Columbia University Press, 2006), p. 8.

[125]. Eddington, A. S., The Nature of the Physical World, (New York: The Macmillan Company, 1929), p. 330. (publicdomain)

[126]. Tillich, P., The Courage To Be, (New Haven: YaleUniversity Press, 1980), p. 23.

[127]. Novak, M., The Experience of Nothingness,

(NewYork: Harper and Row, 1978), pp. 16-17.

[128]. Davies, P., The Origin of Life, (London: Penguin Books, 2003), p. 43.59

[129]. Eddington, A. S., The Nature of the Physical World, (New York: The Macmillan Company, 1929), p. 281-282. (public domain)

[130]. Eddington, A. S., The Philosophy of Physical Science, (New York: Cambridge University Press, 1939), p. 115.

[131]. Russell, B., An Outline of Philosophy (New York: NewAmerican Library, 1974), p. 157.

[132]. Patterson, E., John Dalton and the Atomic Theory, (Garden City, NY: Doubleday and Company, 1970), p. 127.

[133]. Patterson, E., John Dalton and the Atomic Theory, (Garden City, NY: Doubleday and Company, 1970), p. 126.

[134]. Planck, M., Scientific Autobiography and Other Papers, (Westport, Connecticut: Greenwood Press, 1971), p 135.

[135]. Eddington, A. S., The Philosophy of Physical Science, (New York: Cambridge University Press, 1939), p. 20.

[136]. Capra, F., The Tao of Physics, (Boston: ShambhalaPublications, Inc., 2010), p. 287.

[137]. Eddington, A. S., The Philosophy of Physical

Science, (New York: Cambridge University Press, 1939), p. 90.

[138]. Eddington, A. S., The Nature of the Physical World, (New York: The Macmillan Company, 1929), p. 286. (publicdomain)

[139]. Eddington, A. S., The Philosophy of Physical Science, (New York: Cambridge University Press, 1939), p. 116.

[140]. Wilczek, F., The Lightness of Being (New York, BasicBooks, 2008) p. 74.

[141]. Nagel, T., Mind and Cosmos, (New York: OxfordUniversity Press, 2012), p. 160.

[142]. Eddington, A. S., The Philosophy of Physical Science, (New York: Cambridge University Press, 1939), pp. 135-136.

[143]. Capra, F., The Tao of Physics, (Boston: ShambhalaPublications, Inc., 2010), p. 257.

[144]. Holt, J., "Something Faster Than Light?," The NewYork Review of Books , 63:17 (November 10 2016 issue),p.52.

[145]. Skinner, B. F., About Behaviorism (New York: Random House, 1976), pp. 14-50.

[146]. Monod, J., Chance and Necessity (New York: VintageBooks, 1971), p. xi.

[147]. Gelehrter, T., King, R., Ledbetter, D., Nussbaum, R., "Genetics and Molecular Medicine," Medical

Knowledge SelfAssessment IX (USA: American College of Physicians, 1991),pp. 16-17.

[148]. Eddington, A. S., The Philosophy of Physical Science, (New York: Cambridge University Press, 1939), p. 122.

[149]. Eddington, A. S., The Philosophy of Physical Science, (New York: Cambridge University Press, 1939), p. 21.

[150]. Eddington, A. S., The Philosophy of Physical Science, (New York: Cambridge University Press, 1939), p. 119.

[151]. Eddington, A. S., The Philosophy of Physical Science, (New York: Cambridge University Press, 1939), p. 131.

[152]. Eddington, A. S., The Nature of the Physical World, (New York: The Macmillan Company, 1929), p. 271. (publicdomain)

[153]. Nagel, T., Mind and Cosmos, (New York: OxfordUniversity Press, 2012), p. 35.

[154]. Tillich, P., Systematic Theology Vol III, (Chicago: TheUniversity of Chicago Press, 1971), p 24.

[155]. Eddington, A. S., The Nature of the Physical World, (New York: The Macmillan Company, 1929), p. 329. (publicdomain)

[156]. Eddington, A. S., The Nature of the Physical World, (New York: The Macmillan Company, 1929), p. 329. (publicdomain)

[157]. Eddington, A. S., The Nature of the Physical World, (New York: The Macmillan Company, 1929), p 278. (public domain), quoting from Russell, B., Analysis of Matter, (Nottingham, England: Spokesman Books, 2007), p. 320. Online: http://strangebeautiful. com/other-texts/russell -anal -matter.pdf copyright by the Bertrand Russell Peace Foundation

[158]. Schopenhauer, A., The World as Idea, printed in The Philosophy of Schopenhauer, ed. Edman, I., (New York: TheModern Library, 1928), p. 3.

[159]. Rand, Ayn., Anthem

[160]. Nagel, T., Mind and Cosmos, (New York: OxfordUniversity Press, 2012), p. 103.

[161]. Nietzsche, F., The Will To Power, edited by Kaufmann,W., (New York: Random House, 1967), p. 35.

[162]. Eddington, A. S., The Nature of the Physical World, (New York: The Macmillan Company, 1929), p. 271. (publicdomain)

[163]. Popper, K., Objective Knowledge (Oxford: OxfordUniversity Press, 1975), pp. 4-5.

[164]. Eddington, A. S., Space Time and Gravitation: An Outline of the General Relativity Theory, (New York: Cambridge University Press, 1920), p 12., quoting Bertrand Russell in Mysticism and Logic and other Essays (London: Longman, Green and Company, 1925), p. 27.

[165]. DeLong, H., A Profile of Mathematical Logic (Reading,MA: Addison-Wesley, 1970), p. 226.

[166]. Nagel, T., Mind and Cosmos, (New York: OxfordUniversity Press, 2012), p. 105-107.

[167]. Bonhoeffer, D., Ethics, trans. Smith, N. H., (New York:Simon and Schuster, 1995), pp. 17-38.

[168]. Giddens, A., New Rules of Sociological Method, (NewYork: Basic Books, 1976), p. 13.

[169]. Trotsky, L., Dewey, J., Novack, G., Their Morals andOurs (New York: Pathfinder Press, 1973), pp. 48-49.

[170]. Sartre, John-Paul, Being and Nothingness, translated by Barne, H., (New York: Washington Square Press, 1975), p.159. (online edition: http://www.ahandfulofleaves.org/documents/BeingAndNothingness_Sartre.pdf. p. 107.)

[171]. Online interview with Sergiu Celibidache on his philosophy of music: https://youtu.be/SthKs40ClCY.

[172]. Eddington, A. S., Space Time and Gravitation: An Outline of the General Relativity Theory, (New York: Cambridge University Press, 1920), p 46. (public domain -published before 1923)

[173]. Tillich, P., Systematic Theology Vol I, (Chicago: TheUniversity of Chicago Press, 1971), p 274.

[174]. Tillich, P., Systematic Theology Vol I, (Chicago: TheUniversity of Chicago Press, 1971), p 275.

[175]. Tillich, P., Systematic Theology Vol I, (Chicago: TheUniversity of Chicago Press, 1971), p 276.

[176]. Ptolemy, Almagest, the opening epigraph

[177]. Barnes, J., Levels of Life (Toronto: Random HouseCanada, 2013), p. 75.

[178]. Freud, S., Reflections on War and Death , trans. Brill, A. A., Kuttner, A. B., (New York: Moffat, Yard and Co., 1918), p. 7 online www.sophia- project.org/ uploads/1/3/9/5/13955288/freud_waranddeath.pdf

[179]. Rumi, Mystic Odes, 833

[180]. Rilke, R. M., A Year With Rilke , translated and edited by Macy, J., Barrows, A., (New York: Haper-Collins, 2009), p58.

[181]. Tillich, P., The Socialist Decision, translated by F. Sherman (New York, Harper & Row, Publishers, 1977), p 25.

[182]. Planck, M., "Religion and Natural Science" in ScientificAutobiography and Other Papers, (Westport, Connecticut: Greenwood Press, 1971), p 184.

[183]. Marcus Aurelius Antoninus, Meditations, translated byFarquharson, A.S.L (New York, Everyman Library, 1992), p iii, 16.

[184]. Tillich, P., The Courage To Be, (New Haven: YaleUniversity Press, 1980), p. 23.

[185]. Course In Miracles , public domain version online:http://stobblehouse.com/text/ACIM.pdf,

chapter 7, part 1.

[186]. Bonhoeffer, D., Letters and Papers from Prison (London: SCM, 1971), p. 369.

[187]. Gilson, E., Reason and Revelation of the Middle Ages,(New York: Charles Scribner's Sons, 1966), p 96.

[188]. Eddington, A. S., The Nature of the Physical World, (New York: The Macmillan Company, 1929), p. 330. (publicdomain)

[189]. Tillich, P., Systematic Theology Vol I, (Chicago: TheUniversity of Chicago Press, 1971), p 274.

[190]. Wiesel, E., Night (New York, Hill and Wang, 2006),chapter 4.

[191]. The Holy Bible, King James Version. Cambridge edition: 1769; King James Bible Online, (Cambridge University Press, 2017.) www.kingjamesbibleonline. org., Job38:1.

[192]. Marcus Aurelius Antoninus, Meditations, translated by Crossley, H. (London, Macmillan and Co., 1882), p. ix, 30, 40.

[193]. King, M. L., "Paul's Letter to American Christians" sermon 1958, The Papers of Martin Luther King Jr. , ed. Carson, C. (Berkley: University of California Press, 2007), p.345.

[194]. Suzuki, D. T., Outlines of Mahayana Buddhism (New Delhi: Munshiram Manoharlal Publishers Pvt. Ltd., 2014), p113.

[195]. Tillich, P., Systematic Theology Vol I, (Chicago: TheUniversity of Chicago Press, 1971), p 152.

[196]. Bhagavad Gita, translated by Mitchell, S. (New York,Harmony Books, 2000), p 149.

[197]. Cassirer, E., The Metaphysics of Symbolic Forms, translated by Krois, J. (New Haven: Yale University Press,1996), p 15.

[198]. Descartes, R., Discourse on Method and Meditations, translated by Laurence, J.L. (The Liberal Arts Press, The Bobbs-Merrill Company, 1960), Fourth Meditation, p 114.

[199]. Descartes, R., Discourse on Method and Meditations, translated by Laurence, J.L. (The Liberal Arts Press, The Bobbs-Merrill Company, 1960), Fourth Meditation, p 109.

[200]. Eddington, A. S., The Mathematical Theory of Relativity, (Cambridge: At The University Press, 1923), p.196. (public domain)

[201]. Sartre, Jean-Paul, Existentialism and Human Emotions, (New York: Philosophical Library, 1957), p. 50.

[202]. Freeman, K., The Ancilla to the Pre-Socratic Philosophers (Cambridge: Harvard University Press, 1966), p.26.

[203]. Spinoza, B., The Ethics, translated by Elwes, R.H.M. (Philosophy Classics, independently published, 2022), p. 22.

[204]. Simone de Beauvoir, Adieux: A Farewell To Sartre, translated by O'Brien, P., (New York, Pantheon Books, 1984),p. 438.

[205]. Hay, D., The Medieval Centuries (New York, Harperand Row, 1964), p. 56.